DESERT NOTES
REFLECTIONS IN THE EYE OF A RAVEN

RIVER NOTES
THE DANCE OF HERONS

Other Avon Books by
Barry Lopez

WINTER COUNT

Coming Soon

GIVING BIRTH TO THUNDER,
SLEEPING WITH HIS DAUGHTER

BARRY LOPEZ

DESERT NOTES
REFLECTIONS IN THE EYE OF A RAVEN

RIVER NOTES
THE DANCE OF HERONS

AVON BOOKS ▲ NEW YORK

Desert Notes: Reflections in the Eye of a Raven and *River Notes: The Dance of Herons* were originally published as two separate, individual volumes.

"Desert Notes" originally appeared in slightly different form in *Skywriting*; "Coyote and Rattlesnake" originally appeared in *Northwest Review*; "Twilight" appeared in the *North American Review*.

AVON BOOKS
A division of
The Hearst Corporation
105 Madison Avenue
New York, New York 10016

Desert Notes copyright © 1976 by Barry Holstun Lopez
River Notes copyright © 1979 by Barry Holstun Lopez
Front cover photograph courtesy The Stock Market
Published by arrangement with Andrews & McMeel, Inc.
Library of Congress Catalog Card Number: 90-93152
ISBN: 0-380-71110-9

Library of Congress Cataloging in Publication Data:

Lopez, Barry Holstun, 1945–.
    Desert notes: reflections in the eye of a raven; River notes: the dance of herons/Barry Lopez.
        p. cm.
    ISBN 0-380-71110-9 (pbk.)
    I. Lopez, Barry Holstun, 1945–   River notes. 1990. II. Title.
III. Title: River notes.
PS3562.067D4 1990   90-93152
813'.54—dc20   CIP

First Avon Books Trade Printing: September 1990
First Avon Books Mass Market Printing, *Desert Notes*: February 1981
First Avon Books Mass Market Printing, *River Notes*: November 1980

AVON TRADEMARK REG. U.S. PAT. OFF. AND IN OTHER COUNTRIES, MARCA REGISTRADA, HECHO EN U.S.A.

Printed in the U.S.A.

OPM   10 9 8 7 6 5 4 3 2 1

DESERT NOTES

Reflections in the
Eye of a Raven

for Mary and Adrian

CONTENTS

In calling up images of the past, I find that the plains of Patagonia frequently cross before my eyes; yet these plains are pronounced by all wretched and useless.

They can be described only by negative characters; without habitations, without water, without trees, without mountains, they support merely a few dwarf plants. Why then, and the case is not peculiar to myself, have these arid wastes taken so firm a hold on my memory? Why have not the still more level, the greener and more fertile Pampas, which are serviceable to mankind, produced an equal impression?

I can scarcely analyze these feelings: but it must be partly owing to the free scope given to the imagination.

The plains of Patagonia are boundless, for they are scarcely passable, and hence unknown: they bear the stamp of having lasted, as they are now, for ages, and there seems no limit to their duration through future time. If, as the ancients supposed, the flat earth was surrounded by an impassable breadth of water, or by deserts heated to an intolerable excess, who would not look to these last boundaries to man's knowledge with deep but ill-defined sensations?

Charles Darwin
The Voyage of the Beagle, 1836

INTRODUCTION

With the Desert Fathers you have the characteristic of a clean break with a conventional, accepted social context in order to swim for one's life into an apparently irrational void.

THOMAS MERTON

THE LAND DOES NOT GIVE EASILY. THE DESERT IS like a boulder; you expect to wait. You expect night to come. Morning. Winter to set in. But you expect sometime it will loosen into pieces to be examined.

When it doesn't, you weary. You are no longer afraid of its secrets, cowed by its silence. You break away, angry, a little chagrined. You will tell anyone the story: so much time spent for nothing. In the retelling you sense another way inside; you return immediately to the desert. The opening evaporates, like a vision through a picket railing.

You can't get at it this way. You must come with no intentions of discovery. You must overhear things, as though you'd come into a small and desolate town and paused by an open window. You can't learn anything from saguaro cactus, from ocotillo. They are just passing through; their roots, their much heralded dormancy in the dry season, these are only illusions of permanence. They know even less than you do.

7

You have to proceed almost by accident. I learned about a motor vehicle this way.

I was crossing the desert. Smooth. Wind rippling at the window. There was no road, only the alkaline plain. There was no reason for me to be steering; I let go of the wheel. There was no reason to sit where I was; I moved to the opposite seat. I stared at the empty driver's seat. I could see the sheen where I'd sat for years. We continued to move across the desert.

I moved to the back of the vehicle—a large van with windows all around—and sat by the rear doors. I could hear the crushing of earth beneath the wheels. I opened the doors wide and leaned out. I saw the white alkaline surface of the desert slowly emerging from under the sill, as though the van were fixed in space and the earth turning beneath us.

I opened all the doors. The wind blew through.

I stepped out; ran away. When I stopped and turned around the vehicle was moving east. I ran back to it and jumped in. Out the driver's door; in through the back. I got out again, this time with my bicycle, and rode north furiously until the vehicle was only a speck moving on the horizon behind me. I curved back and crossed slowly in front of it. I could hear the earth crumbling under the crush of my rubber tires and the clicketing of my derailleur gears. I lay the bike down and jogged along-side the vehicle, the padding of my sneakers next to the hiss of the rolling tire. I shifted it into neutral through the open door and turned the key off. I sat in it until it came to rest. I walked back for the bicycle.

Until then I did not understand how easily the vehi-cle's tendencies of direction and movement could be abandoned, together with its systems of roads, road signs, and stop lights. By a series of strippings such as this one enters the desert.

When I first came into the desert I was arrested by the space first, especially what hung in a layer just above the dust of the desert floor. The longer I regarded it the clearer it became that its proportion had limits, that it had an identity, like the air around a stone. I suspected that everything I'd come here to find out was hidden inside that sheet of space.

I developed methods of inquiry, although I appeared to be doing nothing at all. I appeared completely detached. I appeared to be smelling my hands cupped full of rocks. I appeared to be asleep. But I was not. Even inspecting an abandoned building at some distance from the desert I would glance over in that direction, alert. I was almost successful. Toward the end of my inquiry I moved with exquisite ease. But I could not disguise the waiting.

One morning as I stood watching the sun rise, washing out the blue black, watching the white crystalline stars fade, my bare legs quivering in the cool air, I noticed my hands had begun to crack and turn to dust.

DESERT NOTES

I KNOW YOU ARE TIRED. I AM TIRED TOO. WILL YOU walk along the edge of the desert with me? I would like to show you what lies before us.

All my life I have wanted to trick blood from a rock. I have dreamed about raising the devil and cutting him in half. I have thought too about never being afraid of anything at all. This is where you come to do those things.

I know what they tell you about the desert but you mustn't believe them. This is no deathbed. Dig down, the earth is moist. Boulders have turned to dust here, the dust feels like graphite. You can hear a man breathe at a distance of twenty yards. You can see out there to the edge where the desert stops and the mountains begin. You think it is perhaps ten miles. It is more than a hundred. Just before the sun sets all the colors will change. Green will turn to blue, red to gold.

I've been told there is very little time left, that we must get all these things about time and place straight. If we don't, we will only have passed on and have changed nothing. That is why we are here I think, to change things. It is why I came to the desert.

Here things are sharp, elemental. There's no one to look over your shoulder to find out what you're doing with your hands, or to ask if you have considered the number of people dying daily of malnutrition. If you've been listening you must suspect that a knife will be very

11

useful out here—not to use, just to look at.

There is something else here, too, even more important: explanations will occur to you, seeming to clarify; but they can be a kind of trick. You will think you have hold of the idea when you only have hold of its clothing.

Feel how still it is. You can become impatient here, willing to accept any explanation in order to move on. This appears to be nothing at all, but it is a wall between you and what you are after. Be sure you are not tricked into thinking there is nothing to fear. Moving on is not important. You must wait. You must take things down to the core. You must be careful with everything, even with what I tell you.

This is how to do it. Wait for everything to get undressed and go to sleep. Forget to explain to yourself why you are here. Listen attentively. Just before dawn you will finally hear faint music. This is the sound of the loudest dreaming, the dreams of boulders. Continue to listen until the music isn't there. What you thought about boulders will evaporate and what you know will become clear. Each night it will be harder. Listen until you can hear the dreams of the dust that settles on your head.

I must tell you something else. I have waited out here for rattlesnakes. They never come. The moment eludes me and I hate it. But it keeps me out here. I would like to trick the rattlesnake into killing itself. I would like this kind of finality. I would like to begin again with the snake. If such a thing were possible, the desert would be safe. You could stay here forever.

I will give you a few things: bits of rock, a few twigs, this shell of a beetle blown out here by the wind. You should try to put the bits of rock back together to form a stone, although I cannot say that all these pieces are from the same stone. If they don't fit together look for others that do. You should try to coax some leaves from

these twigs. You will first have to determine whether
they are alive or dead. And you will have to find out
what happened to the rest of the beetle, the innards.
When you have done these things you will know a little
more than you did before. But be careful. It will occur
to you that these tasks are silly or easily done. This is a
sign, the first one, that you are being fooled.

I hope you won't be here long. After you have finished
with the stone, the twigs and the beetle, other things will
suggest themselves, and you must take care of them. I
see you are already tired. But you must stay. This is the
pain of it all. You can't keep leaving.

Do you hear how silent it is? This will be a comfort
as you work. Do not laugh. When I first came here I
laughed very loud and the sun struck me across the face
and it took me a week to recover. You will only lose time
by laughing.

I will leave you alone to look out on the desert. What
makes you want to leave now is what is trying to kill you.
Have the patience to wait until the rattlesnake kills itself.
Others may tell you that this has already happened, and
this may be true. But wait until you see for yourself,
until you are sure.

THE HOT SPRING

I.

THE MAN WOULD SET OFF LATE IN THE SPRING, AFTER
the dogwood had bloomed, in the blue '58 Chevy pickup
with the broken taillight and the cracked Expando mir-
rors. He would take a thin green sleeping bag and a
blue tarpaulin, a few dishes and a one-burner stove. He
would take his spoon and only cereal to eat and tea to
drink. He would take no books, no piece of paper to
write on.

He would stop only for gas and would pick up no
hitchhikers. He would drive straight through on the two-
lane, blacktop roads, cracked and broken with the freeze
of last winter, without turning the radio on. He would
lift his damp buttocks from the hot naugahyde seat and
let the wind, coming in through the window that was
stuck halfway down, cool him.

It would take seven hours to drive the 278 miles. First,
over the mountains, past the great lava flows at the ridge,
past the slopes of black obsidian glass, down into the
sweet swamp of thick air in the ponderosa forest.

He would drive out then into the great basin over
arroyos and across sage flats dotted with juniper and
rabbit brush, past the fenced squares marked Experi-
mental Station where the government was trying to grow
crested wheat grass, trying to turn the high desert into
grassy fields for bony Herefords with vacant eyes. He
would see few cows. He would see, on a long stretch of

15

road, a golden eagle sitting on a fence post.

There would be more space between the towns and more until there were no towns at all, only empty shacks, their roof ridges bowed, their doors and windows gone.

He would come around the base of another range of mountains, slip down on the southeastern side and drive on a one-lane dirt road along the edge of the alkaline desert for twenty miles until he came to the hot spring. There he would stop. He would stop the truck, but he would leave the motor running to keep the engine cool. He would always arrive by one in the afternoon.

II.

He inhaled the tart, sulphurous fumes rising up from the green reeds, the only bit of green for miles. He watched the spiders spinning webs in the wire grass and the water bugs riding the clots of yellow bubbles. He stared at the bullet-riddled walls of tin that surrounded the sandy basin where the water collected.

When he had seen these things, that they had weathered the winter, the man put the truck in gear and rolled down over the sagebrush and onto the desert floor. He drove out over the dry, bleached soil for a mile before he put the truck in neutral and let it coast to a stop. He was careful with the silence. He could hear his fingers slide over the plastic steering wheel. He could feel the curve of his lips tightening in the dryness.

He took off his clothes, all of them, and put them in a zippered airlines bag on the floor of the truck. Then he put his sneakers back on and went naked across the desert back to the hot spring with a pair of linen socks in his hand. The cool breeze from the mountains raised his flesh into a lattice of pin-pricked hills.

He removed his shoes. He lay on his back in the hot water, his toes grazing the shallow, sandy bottom of the pool. He could hear the water lapping at the entrance to his ears, the weight of water pulling on his hair; he could feel the particles of dust falling off his flesh, floating down, settling on the bottom of the pool; he could feel the water prying at the layers of dried sweat. He concentrated and tried to hear the dirt and sweat breaking away from his body. The tips of his fingers wrinkled, and he stared at the water pooling in the cavity of his chest and falling away as he breathed.

He wanted to stay until the sun set but he couldn't: he could feel himself sinking. He climbed out of the pool and walked out of the roofless tin shelter onto the floor of the desert. The wind began to evaporate the water and his pores closed like frightened mussels and trapped the warmth beneath his skin.

When his feet were dry he put on only the linen socks and left. He could feel the wind eddying up around him like a cloak and his feet barely touched the ground. His eyes felt smoother in their sockets and he could tell, without looking, how his fingers were curled; he could see the muscles of his legs tied beneath his kneecaps, feel the patella gliding over the knot. He felt the muscles anchored on the broad, flat plate of his hipbones and the wind soft deep in the roots of his hair. He felt the pressure of his parting the air as he walked.

When he got back to the truck he poured a cup of water and placed a handful of cereal into an earthen bowl. He ate and looked out across the desert and imagined that he had come to life again.

THE RAVEN

I AM GOING TO HAVE TO START AT THE OTHER END by telling you this: there are no crows in the desert. What appear to be crows are ravens. You must examine the crow, however, before you can understand the raven. To forget the crow completely, as some have tried to do, would be like trying to understand the one who stayed without talking to the one who left. It is important to make note of who has left the desert.

To begin with, the crow does nothing alone. He cannot abide silence and he is prone to stealing things, twigs and bits of straw, from the nests of his neighbors. It is a game with him. He enjoys tricks. If he cannot make up his mind the crow will take two or three wives, but this is not a game. The crow is very accommodating and he admires compulsiveness.

Crows will live in street trees in the residential areas of great cities. They will walk at night on the roofs of parked cars and peck at the grit; they will scrape the pinpoints of their talons across the steel and, with their necks outthrust, watch for frightened children listening in their beds.

Put all this to the raven: he will open his mouth as if to say something. Then he will look the other way and say nothing. Later, when you have forgotten, he will tell you he admires the crow.

The raven is larger than the crow and has a beard of

black feathers at his throat. He is careful to kill only
what he needs. Crows, on the other hand, will search
out the great horned owl, kick and punch him awake,
and then, for roosting too close to their nests, they will
kill him. They will come out of the sky on a fat, hot
afternoon and slam into the head of a dozing rabbit and
go away laughing. They will tear out a whole row of
planted corn and eat only a few kernels. They will def-
ecate on scarecrows and go home and sleep with 200,000
of their friends in an atmosphere of congratulation.
Again, it is only a game; this should not be taken to
mean that they are evil.

There is however this: when too many crows come
together on a roost there is a lot of shoving and noise
and a white film begins to descend over the crows' eyes
and they go blind. They fall from their perches and lie
on the ground and starve to death. When confronted
with this information, crows will look past you and warn
you vacantly that it is easy to be misled.

The crow flies like a pigeon. The raven flies like a
hawk. He is seen only at a great distance and then not
very clearly. This is true of the crow too, but if you are
very clever you can trap the crow. The only way to be
sure what you have seen is a raven is to follow him until
he dies of old age, and then examine the body.

Once there were many crows in the desert. I am told
it was like this: you could sit back in the rocks and watch
a pack of crows working over the carcass of a coyote.
Some would eat, the others would try to squeeze out the
vultures. The raven would never be seen. He would be
at a distance, alone, perhaps eating a scorpion.

There was, at this time, a small alkaline water hole at
the desert's edge. Its waters were bitter. No one but
crows would drink there, although they drank sparingly,
just one or two sips at a time. One day a raven warned
someone about the dangers of drinking the bitter water
and was overheard by a crow. When word of this passed
among the crows they felt insulted. They jeered and

raised insulting gestures to the ravens. They bullied each other into drinking the alkaline water until they had drunk the hole dry and gone blind.

The crows flew into canyon walls and dove straight into the ground at forty miles an hour and broke their necks. The worst of it was their cartwheeling across the desert floor, stiff wings outstretched, beaks agape, white eyes ballooning, surprising rattlesnakes hidden under sage bushes out of the noonday sun. The snakes awoke, struck and held. The wheeling birds strew them across the desert like sprung traps.

When all the crows were finally dead, the desert bacteria and fungi bored into them, burrowed through bone and muscle, through aqueous humor and feathers until they had reduced the stiff limbs of soft black to blue dust.

After that, there were no more crows in the desert. The few who watched from a distance took it as a sign and moved away.

Finally there is this: one morning four ravens sat at the edge of the desert waiting for the sun to rise. They had been there all night and the dew was like beads of quicksilver on their wings. Their eyes were closed and they were as still as the cracks in the desert floor.

The wind came off the snow-capped peaks to the north and ruffled their breath feathers. Their talons arched in the white earth and they smoothed their wings with sleek, dark bills. At first light their bodies swelled and their eyes flashed purple. When the dew dried on their wings they lifted off from the desert floor and flew away in four directions. Crows would never have had the patience for this.

If you want to know more about the raven: bury yourself in the desert so that you have a commanding view of the high basalt cliffs where he lives. Let only your eyes protrude. Do not blink—the movement will alert the raven to your continued presence. Wait until a generation of ravens has passed away. Of the new generation there will be at least one bird who will find you. He will see your eyes staring up out of the desert floor. The raven is cautious, but he is thorough. He will sense your peaceful intentions. Let him have the first word. Be careful: he will tell you he knows nothing.

If you do not have the time for this, scour the weathered desert shacks for some sign of the raven's body. Look under old mattresses and beneath loose floorboards. Look behind the walls. Sooner or later you will find a severed foot. It will be his and it will be well preserved.

Take it out in the sunlight and examine it closely. Notice that there are three fingers that face forward, and a fourth, the longest and like a thumb, that faces to the rear. The instrument will be black but no longer shiny, the back of it sheathed in armor plate and the underside padded like a wolf's foot.

At the end of each digit you will find a black, curved talon. You will see that the talons are not as sharp as you might have suspected. They are made to grasp and hold fast, not to puncture. They are more like the jaws of a trap than a fistful of ice picks. The subtle difference serves the raven well in the desert. He can weather a storm on a barren juniper limb; he can pick up and examine the crow's eye without breaking it.

TWILIGHT

I AM SITTING ON A STORM PATTERN RUG WOVEN OUT of the mind of a Navajo woman, Ahlnsaha, and traded to a man named Dobrey in Winslow, Arizona, for groceries in August 1934.

In the fall of 1936 a Swedish farmer, Kester Vorland, his land gone out from under him in the Depression, leaves his wife and three children in the car and, picking his moment perfectly, steps back into the store to steal the rug while Dobrey is busy in the back with a broken saddle. He trades it the next day in Flagstaff for groceries and $25 cash and moves on to Needles. It is bought later by a young man named Diego Martin who takes it back to San Bernardino, California, with him. He boasts of it to his friends, a piece of shrewd buying. When he is married in 1941 he gives it to his wife and, one flat September night, they make love on it, leaving a small stain that the girl, Yonella, can easily point out but which Diego will not believe, even when she shows him. He believes it is a stain left by an insect; he forbids her to show the rug to anyone after this. He dies in a bar fight in Honolulu on April 16, 1943, a corporal in the Marines. Yonella sells everything. An old woman with red hair and liver spots on her throat pouch named Elizabeth Reiner buys the rug for $45 and takes it home with her to Santa Barbara. In 1951 her daughter comes to visit and her grandson John Charles who is ten begins to covet the rug; when the mother and daughter fall into an argument over something, the older woman angrily gives it to the boy (she snatches it down off the wall) as demonstration of her generosity. She later tells her daughter not to come back again and begins to miss the rug and feel foolish. The boy doesn't care. He vows he will always write her at Christmastime, even if his mother forbids it.

On the train from Los Angeles to Prairie du Chien the boy keeps himself wrapped in the rug like a turtle. He sits on the bed in his underwear with it over his shoulders and watches Nebraska. When he is sixteen John Charles falls in love with Dolores Patherway who is nineteen and a whore. One night she trades him twenty-five minutes for the blanket, but he does not see it this way: it is a gift, the best he can offer, a thing of power. That night she is able to sell it to a Great Lakes sailor for $60. She tells him it is genuine Sioux, there at the battle of the Little Big Horn, and will always bring a good price. The sailor's name is Benedict Langer, from a good Catholic family in Ramapo, New Jersey, and he has never had hard liquor or even VD but in three weeks in the service his father said would make a man of him he has lain in confusion with six different women who have told him he was terrific; he has sensed a pit opening. The day after he buys it Benedict gives the blanket to a friend, Frank Winter, and goes to look for a priest in Green Bay, the football town. In March 1959 Frank mails it to his parents for an anniversary present (it has been in his footlocker for eighteen months and smells like mothballs, a condition he remedies by airing it at night from the signal deck of the *U.S.S. Kissell*). He includes with it a document he has had made up in the ship's print shop to the effect that it is an authentic Pawnee blanket, so his parents will be proud, can put it up on the wall of their retirement home in Boca Raton, Florida, next to the maracas from Guadalajara. They leave it in the box in the hall closet; they do not talk

about it. Mr. Winter confides to his wife in the dark one
night that he doesn't believe in the powers of medicine
men.

On July 17, 1963, Frank Winter dies instantly when
his foot hits a land mine in the Mekong Delta. His father
waits a month before donating the blanket and the boy's
other belongings to Catholic Charities. Father Peter
Donnell, a local priest, a man of some sensitivity, lays
the rug down on brown wall-to-wall carpeting in the
foyer of the refectory of the Catholic Church in Boca
Raton, arranging two chairs and a small table precisely
on it (he likes especially the Ganado red color) before
the Monsignor asks him to remove it. Father Donnell
keeps the rug in his room, spread out flat under his
mattress for a year. He takes it with him when he is
transferred to Ames, Iowa, where it is finally bought in
an Easter bazaar as Father Donnell endures a self-
inflicted purging of personal possessions. It is bought
by antique dealers, Mr. and Mrs. Theodore Wishton
Spanner of Jordan Valley, Oregon (as they sign the reg-
ister). The following winter I buy it from Mrs. Spanner
who tells me the rug has been woven by a Comanche
who learned his craft from a Navajo, that she bought it
on the reservation in Oklahoma. It is certified. I take
the rug home and at dusk I undress and lie down under
it so that it completely covers my body. I listen all night.
I do not hear anything. But in this time I am able to
sort out all the smells buried in the threads and the
sounds still reverberating deep in the fibers. It is what
I have been looking for.

It is this rug I have carefully spread out now, east and
west over the dust. It is only from such a height above
the floor of the desert that one is able to see clearly what
is going on.

The moon has just risen; the sun has just gone down.
There are only a few stars up and a breeze is blowing
up from the south. It smells like wet cottonwood leaves.

This is the best time to see what is happening. Everyone who is passing through will be visible for a short time. Already I have seen the priest with his Bible bound in wolves' fur and the blackbirds asleep in his hair.

I see the woman who smells like sagebrush and her three children with the large white eyes and tattered leggings. I see the boy who rolls in dust like a horse and the legionnaire with the alabaster skin polished smooth by the wind. I see the magnificent jethery loping across the desert like a greyhound with his arms full of oars. I watch cheetahs in silver chariots pulled by a span of white crows. I see the rainbow in arabesques of the wind.

The night gets deeper. I pull down to listen for Ahlnsaha: she is crying in Arizona. This is what she is singing:

> Go to the white rain
> Ta ta ta ta
> Go to the white rain
> Ta ta ta ta
> I see the horses
> Ta ta ta ta
> They are feeding above there.

There is no rain; there are no horses. Her music falls into pieces with her tears in the dust like lies. She smells like your face in wheat.

The moon is up higher, clearing the thin clouds on the horizon.

The two girls with the sun in a spiderweb bag are standing by the mountains south talking with the blue snake that makes holes in the wind with his whistle.

I can smell the heat of the day stuck on the edges of the cracks in the earth like a salt crust after a tide. I lay back and watch the sky. I close my eyes. I run my hands out smooth over the rug and feel the cold rising from the earth. When I come again I will bring a friar's robe with a deep cowl and shoes of jute fiber. I will run like a madman to the west all night until I begin to fall asleep; then I will walk back, being careful to correct for the tilt of the earth, the force of Coriolis, reading my breviary by the precise arrowlight of stars, assured of my destination.

The day hugs the desert floor like a fallen warrior. I am warm. I am alert for any sort of light. I believe there is someplace out there where you can see right down into the heart of the earth. The light there is strong enough to burn out your eyes like sap in a fire. But I won't go near it. I let it pass. I like to know that if I need it, with only a shovel or a small spade, I can begin digging and recall the day.

This time is the only time you will see the turtles massed on the eastern border for the march to the western edge where there is water, and then back the same night to hide in the bushes and smash insects dazed to lethargy in the cold. I have spoken with these turtles. They are reticent about their commitments. Each one looks like half the earth.

This is the only time you can study both of your shadows. If you sit perfectly still and watch your primary shadow as the sun sets you will be able to hold it long enough to see your other shadow fill up when the moon rises like a porcelain basin with clear water. If you turn carefully to face the south you may regard both of them: to understand the nature of silence you must be able to see into this space between your shadows.

This is the only time you will be able to smell water and not mistake it for the smell of a sheet of granite, or confuse it with the smell of marble or darkness. If you are moving about at this time, able to go anywhere you choose, you will find water as easily as if you were looking for your hands. It may take you some hours, even days to arrive at the place, but there will be no mistake about the direction to go once you smell it. The smell of water is not affected by the air currents so you won't need to know the direction of the wind; the smell of water lays along the surface of the earth like a long stick of peeled elmwood.

This is the only time you can hear the flight of the grey eagle over the desert. You cannot see him because he fades with the sun and is born out of it in the morning but it is possible to hear his wings pumping against the columns of warm air rising and hear the slip of the wind in his feathers as he tilts his gyre out over the desert floor. There is nothing out there for him, no rabbits to hunt, no cliff faces to fall from, no rock on which to roost, but he is always out there at this time fading to grey and then to nothing, turning on the wind with his eyes closed. It doesn't matter how high he goes or how far away he drifts, you will be able to hear him. It is only necessary to lie out flat somewhere and listen for the sound, like the wrinkling of the ocean.

The last thing you will notice will be the stones, small bits of volcanic ash, black glass, blue tourmaline, sapphires, narrow slabs of grey feldspar, rose quartz, sheets of mica and blood agate. They are small enough to be missed, laying down in the cracks of the desert floor, but they are the last things to give up the light; you will see them flare and burn like coals before they let go.

It is good to have a few of these kinds of stones with you in a pocket or cupped in your hand before you go to sleep. One man I knew, only for a short time, was sure the stones were more important than anything else; he kept a blue one tied behind his ear. One evening while we were talking he reached over and with a wet finger took alkaline dust and painted a small lightning bolt on his right cheek. I regarded him for more than an hour before it became too dark to see. I rolled myself up in this blanket and slept.

PERIMETER

I.

IN THE WEST, IN THE BLUE MOUNTAINS, THERE ARE creeks of grey water. They angle out of the canyons, come across the brown scratched earth to the edge of the desert and run into nothing. When these creeks are running they make a terrific noise.

No one to my knowledge has ever counted the number, but I think there are more than twenty; it is difficult to be precise. For example, some of the creeks have been given names that, over the years, have had to be given up because a creek has run three or four times and then the channel has been abandoned.

You can easily find the old beds, where the dust has been washed out to reveal a level of rock rubble—cinnabar laced with mercury, fool's gold, clear quartz powder, and fire opal; but it is another thing to find one of the creeks, even when they are full. I have had some success by going at night and listening for the noise.

There is some vegetation in this area; it does not seem to depend on water. The rattlesnakes live here along with the rabbits. When there is any thunder it is coming from this direction. During the day the wind is here. The smells include the hellebore, vallo weed and punchen; each plant puts out its own smell and together they make a sort of pillow that floats a few feet off the ground where they are not as likely to be torn up by the wind.

II.

To the north the blue mountains go white and the creeks become more dependable though there are fewer of them. There is a sort of swamp here at the edge of the desert where the creeks pool and where grasses and sedges grow and the water takes a considerable time to evaporate and seep into the earth. There are some ducks here, but I do not know where they come from or where they go when the swamp dries up in the summer. I have never seen them flying. They are always hiding, slipping away; you will see their tail feathers disappearing in the screens of wire grass. They never quack.

There are four cottonwood trees here and two black locusts. The cottonwoods smell of balsam, send out seeds airborne in a mesh of exceedingly fine white hair, and produce a glue which the bees use to cement their honeycombs. Only one of the cottonwoods, the oldest one, is a female. The leaf stem meets the leaf at right angles and this allows the leaves to twitter and flash in the slightest breeze. The underside of the leaf is a silver green. I enjoy watching this windflash of leaves in strong moonlight.

The black locusts are smaller, younger trees and grow off by themselves a little. They were planted by immigrants and bear sweet smelling pea-like flowers with short, rose-like thorns at the leaf nodes. There are a few chokecherry bushes and also a juniper tree. You can get out of the sun here at noon and sleep. The wind runs down the sides of the cottonwoods like water and cools you.

An old tawny long-haired dog lives here. Sometimes you will see him, walking along and always leaning to one side. There is also part of a cabin made with finished lumber lying on its back; the dark brown boards are dotted with red and yellow lichen and dry as sun-baked, long forgotten shoes.

III.

To the east the white mountains drop off and there is a flat place on the horizon and then the red mountains start. There is almost nothing growing in these mountains, just a little sagebrush. At the base, where they come to the desert, there are dunes, white like gypsum.

Inside the mountains are old creeks that run in circles over the floors of low-ceilinged caves. The fish in these waters are white and translucent; you can see a pink haze of organs beneath the skin. Where there should be eyes there are grey bulges that do not move. On the walls are white spiders like tight buttons of surgical cotton suspended on long hairy legs. There are white beetles, too, scurrying through the hills of black bat dung.

I have always been suspicious of these caves because the walls crumble easily under your fingertips; there is no moisture in the air and it smells like balloons. The water smells like oranges but has no taste. Nothing you do here makes any sound.

You have to squeeze through these red mountains to get around them; you can't walk over them. You have to wedge yourself in somewhere at the base and go in. There is always a moment of panic before you slip in when you are stuck. Your eyes are pinched shut and the heels of your shoes wedge and make you feel foolish.

At night the wind lies in a trough at the base of the red mountains, sprawled asleep over the white sand dunes like a caterpillar. The edge of the desert is most indistinct in this place where the white sand and the alkaline dust blow back and forth in eddies of the wind's breath while it sleeps.

IV.

In the south the red mountains fall away and yellow mountains rise up, full of silver and turquoise rock.

There are plenty of rabbits here, a little rain in the middle of the summer, fine clouds tethered on the highest peaks. If you are out in the middle of the desert, this is the way you always end up facing.

In the south twelve buckskin horses are living along the edge of the yellow mountains. The creeks here are weak; the horses have to go off somewhere for water but they always come back. There is a little grass but the horses do not seem to eat it. They seem to be waiting, or finished. Ten miles away you can hear the clack of their hooves against the rocks. In the afternoon they are motionless, with their heads staring down at the ground, at the little stones.

At night they go into the canyons to sleep standing up.

From the middle of the desert even on a dark night you can look out at the mountains and perceive the differences in direction. From the middle of the desert you can see everything well, even in the black dark of a new moon. You know where everything is coming from.

THE BLUE MOUND PEOPLE

ONCE THERE WAS A PEOPLE HERE WHO NUMBERED, at their greatest concentration, perhaps two hundred. It has been determined by a close examination of their bones and careful reconstruction of muscle tissues that although they looked as we do they lacked vocal cords. They lived in caves ranged in tiers in the bluffs to the east on the far edge of the desert and because of this some of their more fragile belongings, even clothing, can still be examined intact. The scraps of cloth that have been found are most frequently linen, some of them woven of over a thousand threads to the inch, cloth the thickness of human hair. As nearly as can be determined, there were no distinctions in clothing between the sexes; everyone apparently wore similar linen robes of varying coarseness and sandals made of woven sage.

Also found in the caves were the usual implements: mortars and pestles, cooking knives, even some wooden bowls that, like the cloth, are oddly preserved. The knives are curious, made of silver and inlaid with black obsidian glass along the cutting edge. A number of glass and crystal shards have been found in the dirt on the floors of the caves, along with bits of bone china and porcelain. Some intact pieces have been uncovered and the workmanship is excellent. A pair of heavily worked pewter candlesticks together with scraps of beeswax were also located.

The caves, though with separate entrances, are linked by an odd and, it seems, needlessly complicated maze of interconnecting hallways. Nothing has been found in these hallways except where they juncture with caves; here a storage area seems to have existed, a sort of back porch. It has been theorized that the maze itself might have been a defensive network of some sort.

Other than the sharp implements apparently used in the preparation of food, there are no other weapons of any sort to be found. This at first puzzled archeologists, who had determined by an examination of shallow refuse pits that the cave people lived on a mixed and varied diet of meat and vegetables. Not only were no hunting implements found (not even ropes or materials for building snares), there were, it has been determined, too few animals nearby to account for the abundance revealed in an examination of the refuse pits and larder areas. Further complicating the issue of sustenance is the lack of evidence that soil suitable for farming was available to provide the many cultivated varieties of melon, tomato, cucumber, celery and other vegetables for which we have found fossilized seeds. Nor could there have been enough water without some form of irrigation (and there was no river at that time for that) to support such agriculture. In fact, a series of drillings has revealed that only enough water was available to support perhaps sixty to eighty people over the course of a year without exhausting the water table.

Radiocarbon dating has pinpointed the time of inhabitance at 22,000 ± 1430 years BP. Again, a projection of game populations and climatic conditions for this period indicates that the cave people were living a life of apparent plenty in an area that, clearly, could not support such an existence. It has been suggested that these people hunted and farmed abroad but preferred to live at the edge of the desert and traversed great distances in order to do so, but this suggestion has not been taken seriously. The nearest area with sufficient

water and soil suitable for farming lies sixty miles to the
northeast. Also there is this: the major source of meat,
after rabbits and, strangely, geese, was a diminutive antelope, an extremely wary creature so widely scattered
that it could not be effectively hunted by men on foot.
Only very occasionally could such animals be tricked into
running off a cliff or trapped in a piskun. It has been
conjectured that they traded for their food but this is
highly unlikely.

The question of how they provided for themselves
remains unanswered.

Other questions also remain. For instance, no cause
of death has been determined for the 173 sets of remains, but it is believed that they all died within the
period of a year. All but one was arranged in a crypt in
the walls of the caves. The one who was not was found
sitting on the floor with his back against an intricately
woven cedar bark backrest. This man was in his forties
and was apparently working on a piece of beaded cloth
when he died. It has never been suggested where his
white alabaster beads came from.

What these people did is also a mystery; just as there
are no hunting implements, so there are no agricultural
tools. Nor is there evidence of elaborate religious cer-
emonies nor extensive artwork nor are there tools or
ovens to work the glass and metal objects found in the
caves (and it is extremely unlikely that these were ob-
tained in trade as we know of no other cultural group
with such skills in existence at this time).

Some believe that a key to understanding these people
lies in determining the purpose of a series of blue earth
mounds. These mounds of deep blue-grey dust are
about a foot high and are perfectly conical in shape but
for the rounded tops. One was found in each cave and
the remains of four of them have been detected out on
the desert, approximately a mile from the caves. At the
heart of each one, toward the base, a hard white stone
was found, perfectly round, smoother than dry marble,

as if it had been washed for hundreds of years in a creek bed. These stones are gypsum-like but of a different crystalline structure and extremely light. There is some reason to believe that they are the fossilized remains of some sort of organism.

It is for this reason, of course, that these people are referred to as the People of the Blue Earth or the Blue Mound People. They cannot be associated, either geographically or by the level of certain of their crafts with any of their supposed contemporaries. And a number of questions continue to pose themselves. In spite of their anatomical inability to speak, we find no evidence of any other system of communication. No paintings, no writing, no systems of marking, no sequences of any sort. And there is, of course, no source for the linen cloth. There are no objects which might be called toys or evidence of any games, although several lute-like instruments have been found. Almost everything else is quite common in design but the materials from which some things have been made are unusual. There are, as I have indicated, pieces of china and glass, even sterling silver, but, as I have noted, no evidence of their fabrication. A careful sifting of cave soils has revealed fragments of oak and leather furniture but no evidence of fire pits, as, indeed there was at that time apparently no wood or other fuel close by. As nearly as can be determined, food was prepared on rock slabs outside the caves with perhaps some glass device to concentrate the rays of the sun. Inside the caves there was, it seems, no source of heat.

A single scrap of papyrus-like paper has been found and objects for which no explanation has been set forth (among them a smooth red sandstone disc and an enormous turtle shell) have also been appearing.

Further analysis of the cave soils and a closer examination of the surrounding area continues, but you can see the problem. We are dealing here with a people entirely out of the order of things and, for this reason, we should be forgiven any sort of speculation. An artist with an eastern museum, for example, has completed a series of drawings based on anatomical studies; he has given these people blue-grey skin and white hair with soft grey eyes. His pictures are very striking; the eyes have a kind, penetrating quality to them. He is perfectly free to do this.

But I have my own ideas.

The alkaline desert was here at the time these people were, this I have on the best scientific authority, even though the area surrounding the desert was swamp-like and no reasons can be given for the existence of a desert in this area at that time. It is obvious to me, then, that these people lived with some unusual arrangement in this desert; conditions were harsh in the extreme, and their food and water (not to mention linen, silver, and glass) had to come from somewhere else. I do not think it facetious at all to suggest, especially to anyone who has seen these caves, then, that in exchange for food, water, and other necessities these people were bound up in an unusual relationship with the desert. I have examined the caves closely enough myself to have determined that these were both a comfortable people, free from want, and a sedentary or perhaps even meditative people. This seems most reasonable.

I think it will be found too that the blue mounds with their white stone hearts have more to do with the desert than they have to do with the people alone. I think they might even be evidence of a bond between the people and the desert. I assume that the desert was the primary force in this relationship, but I could be wrong. It could have been the people who forged this relationship; we have no way of knowing exactly what they were capable of doing. Perhaps they were blue-skinned, and each had the thought of the desert at his heart, like the white stone in the blue earth, maybe this is the meaning. Perhaps this is what they are trying to say, that the desert is only a thought. I don't know.

There have been other suggestions, of course, mostly of a religious nature, but it is all conjecture. Many, of course, have avoided any mention of the blue mounds. In the years since I first discovered the caves I have noticed that they have been shifting a little to the north each year although the wall they are set in seems solid. I am apparently the only one to have noticed this. I have also been here recently when the caves were gone.

CONVERSATION

YOU ARE GOING TO LOSE YOUR SHIRT THEN.

No.

Let me ask you this: how are you going to get on out here? You told me you are sixty-one. You are very active, I can see that. Still, there is water to be carried every day, there is wood to be gathered, food—how long can you reasonably expect to live here with such limited resources? From where we sit I don't even see a juniper tree.

Have you ever seen a spider make a web? The thread comes out through little holes right above his ass. It is so thin you can hardly see it. He makes a trap for the bugs in the air. Before the web is made, before the bug is caught, the bug knows nothing of webs. It's as if the bug and the web didn't exist. The bug dies, he is eaten, he becomes material for a new web. The wind tears the old web down.

The point, then, is to hold still, to stay in one place? Yes.

To wait. Is one supposed to wait for . . . what? Do you wait for something, for some *thing* to appear? Someone to come? Are you suggesting a mental thing?

You wait for yourself.

I'm already here.

No. Not really. You are stretched out like a string all over the place. The end of the string is here, the rest is

39

there and there, back there in the mountains, on the
other side. You must reel in the string, you must roll
yourself up in a ball and then unravel yourself out here
where you have the room and the clear light to study
the condition of the threads.

Once you have the string all laid out, once you have
repaired the worn pieces, you will establish certain
points. Between these points you will line out the string
until you have made a web, strong, very taut. The impact
of a breeze at one edge will be felt at another. Sunlight
will bounce when it hits, as though it were a trampoline.
The sunlight will turn somersaults and you will know
you have made the thing well. Then listen for the wind.
The sound of the wind on the threads.

I must tell you this. I think this is bullshit.

It's bullshit because you are afraid your string will be
too short. You are afraid it is too frayed, that you will
be making knots all the time, that your web will be small
and ridiculous.

I don't trust metaphors.

I am not talking metaphors. I am telling you the truth.

THE SCHOOL

LOOK: FROM THE SIZE OF THE HOLES YOU CAN GUESS at the size of the bullets. These tiny ones, .22's. These, this cluster here, .30–30's maybe. Over here...this bunch in the floor. Eleven .44 magnums I think. Maybe a .45 automatic. Maybe whoever...maybe who made these holes in the floor was shooting *at* something, a rattlesnake. We have a lot of rattlesnakes. They come in here to get out of the sun.

All these holes scattered in the walls are from hunters. They come by looking for coyotes and rabbits and shoot at this because it's the only thing around. You'd never be able to tell what kind of bullets those holes are from, only if the shots came from inside or outside. That's a shotgun blast.

In the back here where the kitchen was...here...was this stove. Porcelain-faced, enameled handles, nickel-plated moulding. You can see what it was like. You can make out down here where someone's taken the name plate: see where the light affected the color of the metal over a period of years? Look at the way the oven door is caved in, like an old mouth. Shotgun did that. Four or five blasts with a shotgun. Look at this where they took the nickel-plated supports for the bread warmer, just hammered them off. Not even a wrench or a screwdriver. Well—maybe someone came by and scared them off.

This open space here is where the rear doors used to be, double doors of oak. I remember there were big brown knots in there, chocolate-colored and bigger than your fists. The brass plate where the latch slid across and the brass throw bolts for the second door both ran with the grain of the wood. (Don't step in that dog mess there.) They brought those doors over from the valley in 1921. Connie Whalen's father who owned the mines bought them.

These places were where the casement windows were. We'd open them in the hot weather and the front doors to get cross ventilation. There were fourteen panes of glass to each one. That was one of my jobs, to clean them. There's part of one of the window lattices out there in the rabbit brush.

This back room was for storage and where Miss Lamse kept some of her things. There was a day bed here and a little teak table over there that Miss Lamse brought back from San Francisco one summer. This plaster wall was put in after the building was built—you can see it's not as carefully done—look there where someone's pulled the plaster away how the lath has been set crooked. They did that when I was in the fourth grade on account of a fire regulation or something.

There was a door here of course. It had a steel handle that heated up in the afternoon because of the way the sun was on it coming through the windows. I can remember it that well. So much grease on these hinges they didn't make a sound; but the back doors squeaked. You know—here, look at this: even the window latches are gone. I knew they broke the glass and tore out the framing (you can see where they started a fire in the corner over there with some of the framing) but here somebody has gone to the trouble to take out the latches. Well, maybe they're worth something now. The windows were put in in 1922, the same year they put the building up. It all dates from 1922 except the plaster wall. (Look here at how hard this piece of hot dog is.)

I remember one morning Miss Lamse was having us clean up before we went home for Christmas. We were working on the desks (they used to be here, in rows, bolted to the floor); we were oiling the wood and the boys were scrubbing the floor—it was a hardwood floor, maybe maple, not this, this was the underfloor. Wait, here's a piece of the old floor. I don't know. Maybe it was maple. Well: we were oiling the desks and the boys were doing the floor to look nice for Christmas, and my best friend, Janet Ribbe, was doing the front windows, four to a side, when we heard Billy Wald screaming in the back room. Someone had hung up five dead rats on a string in the closet back there and spilled the guts out all over the floor. I think Tom Woodson did it but we never knew because Billy left school after that. He was smaller than the other boys, with anemia or something. I always worried about him. Janet Ribbe got sick to her stomach and went home. The boys cleaned it up and threw it all in the bushes. It was about two years later that Billy's father got drunk and shot him.

There were double doors here at the front too. Oak, like the others, and just as shiny, but the throw bolts and the handle were steel, not brass.

I remember the last time I was here when it was nice was when I graduated. Michael Peake and I were both graduated at the same time and went over to Cooley to the high school. That left nineteen here that year. The classes got smaller and smaller and about ten years later, oh, I don't know, maybe twelve, was the last class. By then the cinnabar was gone and the mine was shut down. Most of the people moved out to Cooley or over to Pilot Rock to work in the cement factory.

From then on the building was empty. Mr. Boeken, the county school superintendent, came and got the bell. He was going to give it to a school back east but I think he finally sold it to a museum. One night about seven years ago somebody threw a rope around the little cupola where the bell used to be and pulled it off with a pickup truck or something. By then people had been coming here for years, kids throwing rocks, out-of-state tourists. I don't know where the desks went. Or the books. Miss Lamse had about seventy-five books on a shelf at the back of the room that she left there when she died. There was a stove heater in the main room that's gone. I hope somebody used that maple from the floor. Mr. Whalen brought those boards two hundred miles on the train.

When the sun comes around this afternoon it will be an awful smell in here.

I come over sometimes and try and clean it out, burn up the garbage. I don't know what for. The last time I came over was about five years ago. The trouble with it, right from the beginning, was that it was too far away. The men put it up halfway between the town and the mines, thirty-one miles each way. They sank a well over there where that twisted thing is coming up out of the ground. But nothing ever grew up here, even when we planted. (Look there, down on the desert, at the size of that twister.) In this dry air it'll be a long time before it falls down. They'll have to push it over with a truck or something before they get rid of it.

THE WIND

SHE IS LYING ON HER SIDE IN THE DUST; SHE IS SIGHT-ing along the curve of the desert floor. She is looking out underneath the round polished belly of an ant; the sun is pinging in the creases of his body as though he were made in sections of brown opaque glass. He is rolling a grain of white granite.

The granite cinder is half the size of the ant; it hangs at the lip of a crack. The ant pushes the boulder over the lip; she waits. She lays her ear tighter to the earth. She hears the boulder crashing to the bottom of the crack. She sees the ant slip into the crevice and disappear. She listens. She cannot hear him. She cannot hear him working his way down between the walls of the chasm. He is too careful.

She rolls over on her back. She closes her eyes and puts her hands out flat on her belly and pulls the warm dry air in through her nose and lets it puff out the sacks of her lungs until they are stiff against the inside of her ribs and there is a tingling across the top of her thighs. She imagines her hair slipping into the cracks beneath her, the long shiny black hair rolling like quicksilver off itself and over the alkaline dust and cascading down into the cracks, winding under the earth until her head is bound there like a rock pinned beneath a spider web. She feels a single drop of water bead on her forehead.

It rolls over the bridge of her nose and across her cheek and evaporates.

She can feel the air bending like water around the soles of her feet and can feel it wash up her legs and pool in her belly, running back down through the dark hair and piling between her thighs; feel it moving in twirls up over her ribs, rushing up across her breasts, lying in the pocket of her throat, flowing up over her ears like hands burying in her hair; coming up the side of her leg, around below her hip under her back where there is space between her and the earth, back across her chest and gone, over her arm, tingle, finger, stretch, gone. Tongues of air roping like coils, water brushing dry leaving all the pores of her flesh puckered. With her head to one side she can see it touch out on the desert floor, gone.

She closes her eyes and lays her hands back on her belly.

The ant emerges from the crevice, his antenna filtering the air. He turns around and pulls a sage twig out of the crack. He sets off backwards and the spurs of the twig scratch the dust as he tugs. The noise alerts her; she turns to watch. The ant pulls the sage twig in jerks, levering against a boulder, twisting, until he has the twig at the edge of another crack. She rolls over on her side to place her ear tight against the white earth. He gives the twig a push and she hears it crash like a log batoning down the walls of a shale canyon tearing the earth loose. The ant slips into the crevice and she listens. She cannot hear him.

She rolls over on her stomach and lays her hands flat against the earth and shuts her eyes. She feels the prickling at the bottom of her spine as the moisture evaporates. The light covers her and she can feel its weight against the back of her legs; she can feel the thin blonde hairs on her arms absorbing it. A pressure against her ribs. Up over her back and the tiny hairs fold under the coming weight like rolling wheat sheening the light. It pools in the dimples of her flesh and washes out over her legs to her ankles and splashes over her heels and down over the soles of her feet and pushes against her toes. It moves through her hair pulling it up from her back and washing it over her shoulders, fluffing it flashing in the white light. It curves around to her face and she can feel it curve in the corner of her eye and run out over her nose vibrating the hairs on her cheeks. It tunnels up between her breasts and is gone.

She opens her eyes. She can feel the corner of her mouth wet against the earth. She folds her arms across her back and pushes her body against the weight. She rolls on her side and pulls her knees up. The sun blinks in the fold of her belly. The brown nipple of her white breast rests against a crack in the earth.

The ant is wrestling the husk of a seed. She watches him. He pulls the seed into the shade of a grey stone and leans against it. She can see the swirl of dust snaking over the desert floor toward them. It takes a long time, stopping and disappearing, then starting again, puffing the dust with sighs; the sun begins to fall before the swirl arrives. It comes suddenly over the grey stone like a wave breaking, bowls the seed from the ant's grasp into a foreign crevice and tumbles the ant away. Then it flattens out. It evaporates. It brushes her hips.

The girl rises to her knees and watches the sun balance on the serrated ridge of the mountains. She puts on her clothes.

The ant emerges slowly from a cul-de-sac of dust. He walks across the desert. He disappears into the crevice after the seed.

The girl runs her fingers through her hair like combs and swings it free from her back. She puts on a jacket and twines her arms across her chest and feels the tingle on her thighs where the sun has lain. She fans her hands to a fire of small twigs. Her breath fogs. The puff of hair between her legs is kinked with warmth.

She is asleep. The ant emerges from the crack in the floor of the desert. He has the seed. The yellow light of the full moon glints on his round smooth belly.

COYOTE AND RATTLESNAKE

ONE TIME COYOTE WAS OUT HUNTING AND HE MET Rattlesnake. Rattlesnake was lying in the shadow of a rock at the edge of the desert.

"Coyote, where are you going?"

"I am hunting. I am looking for a fat rabbit. What are you doing?"

"I am waiting for mice."

Coyote sat down on a rock. He filled his mouth with air until his cheeks bulged, then let it leak out one corner of his mouth in a sort of whistling sigh.

"I'm getting tired of looking for food all the time, Rattlesnake. I spend too much time hunting. There are other things I would like to do."

"The winter is almost over. Spring is coming. There will be plenty of rabbits."

"Are you telling me you are doing well? I've seen you every day, waiting for mice. You catch nothing. Can't you see this is foolish?"

"It's the way things are."

"Oh I have no time for this sort of nonsense. I must be going."

Coyote only went off a little distance. He reached down and took a handful of pebbles and rolled them back and forth in his hand. He began flipping the pebbles casually at small targets, as though he were waiting for someone to come along or something to happen. He came back to where Rattlesnake was hidden.

"Rattlesnake, tell me, do you really mean to go on like this year after year? Doing exactly as you are told?"

"How is that, Coyote?"

"Akasitah has said how we should live, that the coyote will hunt rabbits, that he will die at the hands of Shisa. He has said that the rattlesnake will live on the ground where he can see nothing and that he too will die at the hands of the Shisa. Who are the Shisa that I must hunt rabbits and step in traps as though I had no eyes? Who are the Shisa that you are beaten with sticks when they find you? We have all done as Akasitah said we should. But Akasitah is the friend of the Shisa. He is the enemy of all others."

"It is the other way around, Coyote."

"Rattlesnake, I have always believed you were the one who saw things best. When times were very bad you always made us see that in time things would be better. But you are wrong now. I have watched the Shisa. They are changing. They have become worse. I have watched you wait for mice. I have looked for rabbits. There are no rabbits. I am going to see Akasitah."

Coyote flung the few pebbles he had left onto the ground and left.

"I will see you when you come back," said Rattlesnake. He watched Coyote go. He watched for mice.

Akasitah lived in a white cloud at the top of a mountain that rose from the desert. The climb was long and very difficult. Coyote cut his feet on the rocks and cut the flesh of his hands. He fell exhausted on his face when he reached the top. He did not move for a very long time. When he opened his eyes he saw that the top was flat and covered with grass. It was thicker than any grass he had ever heard about. In the middle there was a lake. The water was black. There was an otter there.

You have come to see Akasitah about a new way of life, said the otter. Coyote could hear him very well even though he stood far away by the lake and was looking off the other way. First you must purify yourself, continued Otter.

"What shall I do," said Coyote, not knowing if he could be heard.

You must build a small fire of twigs and sit there by it through the night remembering all you can of your life. In the morning when you see Akasitah at first light you must say what it is you have to say quickly. You cannot come back again another time and say it again. If you are even a little afraid, Akasitah will go away. You will spend the rest of your days looking over your shoulder, running a little. If there is a trick in your heart wrapped in pride, Akasitah will take away the middle of all your thoughts. He will leave you only with the ends. I tell you this, Coyote: if you do not know why you are here, go home. In the morning it will be too late.

Coyote did not know what to think. He wanted to leave. Surely it was not this serious, only a little talking with Akasitah. He thought of the long way up. Rattlesnake would laugh at him. He would stay.

Coyote collected twigs and made the fire. The night grew colder. There was no wind. Still it got colder. The fire gave no heat and consumed no wood. Coyote curled up to keep himself warm as best he could. And he thought. He thought of all he had seen of the Shisa. He had seen their cities from the mountains south of the desert. He could see beyond the curve of the earth from those mountains. He had watched the land change under the hand of Shisa. But this is not what bothered him. In the old days the Shisa had planted, they had put things back. Now they planted nothing, they returned nothing. Each winter there were fewer rabbits. Something could not come from nothing. Each day the Shisa came closer to the desert. It could not go on forever. They had changed it. They had broken the circle and made it straight like a stick.

Coyote watched the stars. He thought of the things in the desert. He thought of Rattlesnake waiting for the mice.

It was hard for Coyote to concentrate in the cold but he spent the night in thought. He remembered the day the Shisa had come loping over the shrub hills toward the desert. They came across a gully and it was full of rattlesnakes. They yelled and beat the snakes to death with sticks. Long after the snakes were dead they beat the snakes and threw them away, kicked them under the bushes. One of them, who was a little wiser, took this as a sign and led the rest of the Shisa away.

He remembered the time the Shisa had cracked open the sacred mountain with a great machine and taken the blue heart of the mountain away in chains. That is when he moved to the desert. He knew it would only be a short time after that before they came. The wise ones were dead. In a little while he would have to walk into the trap, as though he could not see. That is what Akasitah had ordered. In the morning he would tell Akasitah it was no good.

Coyote watched the fire and listened to the stiff air resting on the tips of the thick grass until the sun rose and it lifted away.

When the first light came the fire burned itself out as though it were the sun setting. Coyote looked to the west for the last star in the black sky, to the north for Akasitah's white cloud, to the red mountains in the east, and to the south where he saw a sign of a good day in the yellow light.

Otter was standing far away by the edge of the lake. A wind came up and rippled the water. Coyote watched him but Otter did not move. Finally Otter said, Go a little to the north and wait.

Akasitah was there. Coyote could feel the warm spot in the wind. He began talking.

"Akasitah, I have come here to ask you to change your

mind. Below it is chaos because of the Shisa. In a while
there will be no place to go. I and all my friends, even
the mountains, they will be taken away by the Shisa. It
is said that you are wise and fair. How is it that the Shisa
have come to this? Must I always be a coyote to the Shisa?
Can I not be who I am? I ask you to change things. Let
me walk out of the traps. Let Rattlesnake up off the
ground so he can see something coming. Let these things
happen or we will be no more. There will be nothing
left. The Shisa will take even the desert."

There was a space in the wind.

Coyote, you see like a man with only one eye. The
Shisa are like a great boulder that has broken away from
the side of a mountain. The boulder makes a great noise
as it comes down the side of the mountain. It tears away
great chunks of earth and rock and breaks the trees like
twigs, throwing up a cloud of dust against the sun and
you are afraid for your life. There is no need to be
afraid. It only seems this way because you have never
known the world without the Shisa. You have spent your
life under the boulder. I understand your fear.

Once there were no Shisa at all. When Stah-mi-atlosan
sent me here I found the Shisa trapped inside the flowers
before dawn. They asked to be set free and I put the
sun in the sky and set them free. The rest you know. I
tell you this, Coyote: they are like a boulder fallen off
a mountain. Soon they will hit the earth at the bottom
of the mountain and roll out into the desert leaving a
little trail in the dust. The boulder will come to a
stop. You can sleep on it at night. Do not worry. Go.

"Akasitah!" called Coyote. The warm spot in the wind
was gone. Otter was gone. It was quiet. It took Coyote
the rest of the day to get to the bottom of the mountain.

When he got to the desert he found Rattlesnake in
the same place and even though it was the middle of
the night he sat down and related everything that had
happened and asked Rattlesnake his opinion.

"He told you everything there is to know," said Rattlesnake after a while.

"Still it is not clear to me."

"It is like this," said Rattlesnake. "The Shisa have become so large they are moving back into themselves. They have become like a storm turned inside out, that hurls lightning into itself until it is very small and then there is nothing."

"How can you be sure of this?"

"You must watch, Coyote. You are always going off somewhere; that is why you understand nothing. When the storm comes across the hills toward the desert, watch how it turns itself into nothing. It goes over the desert like a small wind. These things are everywhere, Coyote, if you will open your eyes."

Coyote stood up and walked off a little ways and stopped.

"Where are you going, Coyote?"

"I am going to hunt for rabbits."

Coyote went off to the highest hill he could find and sat down with his back against a rock. He scanned the horizon for a cloud and when he found one he settled down to wait.

He wondered if Rattlesnake had ever lied.

DIRECTIONS

I WOULD LIKE TO TELL YOU HOW TO GET THERE SO
that you may see all this for yourself. But first a warning:
you may already have come across a set of detailed in-
structions, a map with every bush and stone clearly
marked, the meandering courses of dry rivers and other
geographical features noted, with dotted lines put down
to represent the very faintest of trails. Perhaps there
were also warnings printed in tiny red letters along the
margins, about the lack of water, the strength of the
wind and the swiftness of the rattlesnakes. Your confidence in these finely etched maps is understandable, for
at first glance they seem excellent, the best a man is
capable of; but your confidence is misplaced. Throw
them out. They are the wrong sort of map. They are
too thin. They are not the sort of map that can be followed by a man who knows what he is doing. The coyote,
even the crow, would regard them with suspicion.

There is, I should warn you, doubt too about the
directions I will give you here, but they are the very best
that can be had. They will not be easy to follow. Where
it says left you must go right sometimes. Read south for
north sometimes. It depends a little on where you are
coming from, but not entirely. I am saying you will have
doubts. If you do the best you can you will have no
trouble.

(When you get there you may wish to make up a map

for yourself for future reference. It is the only map you
will ever trust. It may consist of only a few lines hastily
drawn. You will not have to hide it in your desk, taped
to the back of a drawer. That is pointless. But don't leave
it out to be seen, thinking no one will know what it is.
It will be taken for scribble and thrown in the waste-
basket or be carefully folded and idly shredded by a
friend one night during a conversation. You might want
to write only a set of numbers down in one corner of a
piece of paper and underline them. When you try to
find a place for it—a place not too obvious, not too well
hidden so as to arouse suspicion—you will begin to understand the futility of drawing maps. It is best in this
case to get along without one, although you will find
your map, once drawn, as difficult to discard as an un-
finished poem.)

First go north to Tate. Go in the fall. Wait in the bus
station for an old man with short white hair wearing a
blue shirt and khaki trousers to come in on a Trailways
bus from Lanner. You cannot miss him. He will be the
only one on the bus.

Take him aside and ask him if he came in from Molnar. Let there be a serious tone to your words, as if you
sensed disaster down the road in Molnar. He will regard
you without saying a word for a long time. Then he will
laugh a little and tell you that he boarded the bus at
Galen, two towns above Molnar.

His name is Leon. Take him to coffee. Tell him you
are a journalist, working for a small paper in North
Dakota, that you are looking for a famous desert that
lies somewhere west of Tate, a place where nothing has
ever happened. Tell him you wish to see the place for
yourself.

If he believes you he will smile and nod and sketch a
map for you on a white paper napkin. Be careful. The
napkin will tear under the pressure of his blunt pencil
and the lines he draws may end up meaning nothing at
all. It is his words you should pay attention to. He will

seem very sure of himself and you will feel a great trust
go between you. You may never again hear a map so
well spoken. There will be a clarity in his description
such that it will seem he is laying slivers of clear glass
on black velvet in the afternoon sun. Still, you will have
difficulty remembering, especially the specific length of
various shadows cast at different times of the day. Listen
as you have never listened before. It will be the very best
he can do under the circumstances.

Perhaps you are a step ahead of me. Then I should
tell you this: a tape recorder will be of no use. He will
suspect it and not talk, tell you he must make connections
with another bus and leave. Or he will give you directions
that will bring you to your death. Make notes if you
wish. Then take the napkin and thank him and go.

You will need three or four days to follow it out. The
last part will be on foot. Prepare for this. Prepare for
the impact of nothing. Get on a regimen of tea and
biscuits and dried fruit. On the third or fourth day, when
you are ready to quit, you will know you are on your
way. When your throat is so thick with dust that you
cannot breathe you will be almost halfway there. When
the soles of your feet go numb with the burning and
you cannot walk you will know that you have made no
wrong turns. When you can no longer laugh at all it is
only a little further. Push on.

It will not be as easy as it sounds. When you have
walked miles to the head of a box canyon and find yourself with no climbing rope, no pitons, no one to belay
you, you are going to have to improvise. When the dust
chews a hole in your canteen and sucks it dry without a
sound you will have to sit down and study the land for
a place to dig for water. When you wake in the morning
and find that a rattlesnake has curled up on your chest
to take advantage of your warmth you will have to move
quickly or wait out the sun's heat.

You will always know this: others have made it. The
man who gave you the map has been here. He now lives

in a pleasant town of only ten thousand. There are no large buildings and the streets are lined with maples and a flush of bright flowers in the spring. There is a good hardware store. There are a number of vegetable gardens—pole beans and crisp celery, carrots, strawberries, watercress and parsley and sweet corn—growing in backyards. The weather is mixed and excellent. Leon has many friends and he lives well and enjoys himself. He rides Trailways buses late at night, when he is assured of a seat. He can make a very good map with only a napkin and a broken pencil. He knows how to avoid what is unnecessary.

RIVER NOTES

The Dance of Herons

for Sandy

Contents

INTRODUCTION

I AM EXHAUSTED. I HAVE BEEN STANDING HERE FOR days watching the ocean curl against the beach, and have sunk very gradually over all these hours to the sand where I lie now, worn out with the waiting. At certain moments, early in the morning most often, before sunrise, I have known exactly what I was watching the water for—but at this hour there is no light, it is hard to see, and so the moment passes without examination.

I do not consider this cruel, nor am I discouraged. I have been here too long.

In the predawn hours I watch the sky, the small distant suns, as winter comes on, of Orion and Canis Major shining above the southern horizon. I can easily imagine a planet among them on the surface of which someone is standing alone in a clearing trying to teach himself to whistle, and is being watched by large birds that look like herons. (I reach out and begin to dig in the sand, feeling for substance, for stones in the earth to hold onto: I might suddenly lose my own weight, be blown away like a duck's breast feather in the slight breeze that now tunnels in my hair.)

I stand back up, resume the watch. I know what I'm looking for. I wait.

I do not know what to do with the weariness, with the exhaustion. I confess to self-delusion. I've imagined myself walking away at times, as though bored or defeated,

63

but contriving to leave enough of myself behind to observe any sign, the slightest change. I would seem to an
observer to be absorbed in a game of string figures between my fingers, inattentive, when in fact I would be
alert to the heartbeats of fish moving beyond the surf.
But these ruses only added to the weariness and seemed,
in the end, irreverent.

I have been here, I think, for years. I have spent nights
with my palms flat on the sand, tracing the grains for
hours like braille until I had the pattern precisely, could
go anywhere—the coast of Africa—and recreate the
same strip of beach, down to the very sound of the water
on sea pebbles out of the sound of my gut that has been
empty for years; to the welling of the wind by vibrating
the muscles of my thighs. Replications. I could make
you believe you heard sandpipers walking in the darkness at the edge of a spent wave, or a sound that would
make you cry at the thought of what had slipped through
your fingers. When tides and the wind and the scurrying
of creatures rearrange these interminable grains of sand
so that I must learn this surface all over again through
the palms of my hands, I do. This is one of my confi-
dences.

I have spent much of my time simply walking.
Once I concentrated very hard on moving soundlessly
down the beach. I anticipated individual grains of sand
losing their grip and tumbling into depressions, and I
moved at that moment so my footfalls were masked. I
imagined myself in between these steps as silent as stone
stairs, but poised, like the heron hunting. In this way I
eventually became unknown even to myself (looking
somewhere out to sea for a flight of terns to pass). I
could then examine myself as though I were an empty
abalone shell, held up in my own hands, held up to the
wind to see what sort of noise I would make. I knew the
sound—the sound of fish dreaming, twilight in a still

pool downstream of rocks in a mountain river.

I dreamed I was a salmon, listening to the noise of water in my dreaming, and in this way returned, moving in the cool evening air wrapped in a camouflage of sound down the beach (over a wide floor of gray-streaked Carrara marble, naked) down the beach (my skin taut, each muscle enunciated as smooth and dense beneath the skin as marble) as silent as snowing.

There are birds here.

I hold in my heart an absolute sorrow for birds, a sorrow so deep that at the first light of day when I shiver like reeds clattering in a fall wind I do not know whether it is from the cold or from this sorrow, whether I am even capable of feeling such kindness. I believe yes, I am.

One rainy winter dawn I stood beneath gray clouds with my arms upstretched, dripping in my light cotton clothes in the familiar ritual, staring at the sand at my feet, about to form a prayer, when I felt birds alight. I felt first the flutter of golden plovers against my head, then black turnstones landing soft as butterflies on my arms, and red phalarope with their wild arctic visions, fighting the wind to land, prickling my shoulders with their needling grip. Their sudden windiness, the stiff brushing of wings, the foreign voices—murrelets alighting on my arms, blinking, blinking yellow eyes, sanderlings, whimbrels, and avocets jumping at my sides. Under them slowly, under heavy eider ducks, beneath the weight of their flapping pleading, I began to go down. As I came to my knees I could feel such anguish as must lie unuttered in the hearts of far-ranging birds, the weight of visions draped over their delicate bones.

Beneath the frantic, smothering wingbeats I recalled the birds of my childhood. I had stoned a robin. I thought the name given the kittiwake very funny. The afternoon of the day my mother died I lay on my bed wondering if I would get her small teakwood trunk with the beautiful brass fittings and its silver padlock. I coveted it in cold contradiction to my show of grief. Feeling someone watching I rolled over and through the window saw sparrows staring at me all explode like buckshot after our eyes met and were gone.

When I awoke the sky had cleared. In the damp sea air I could smell cedar pollen. I washed in a freshwater pool where a river broke out of the shore trees, ran across the beach, and buried itself in the breakers. I took talum roots at the pool's edge and crushed them against the native stone to make a kind of soap and began to wash. I washed the ashes of last night's fire from my hands and washed away a fear of darkness I was now heir to, sleeping alone and exposed on the broad beach. I moved out deeper into the stream, working up a lather in the cold water, scrubbing until my skin shouted with the cold and the rubbing, moving like a man who could dance hard and well alone.

I began each day like this, as though it were the last. I know the last days will be here, where the sun runs into the ocean, and that I will see in a movement of sea birds and hear in the sound of water beating against the earth what I now only imagine, that the ocean has a sadness beyond even the sadness of birds, that in the running into it of rivers is the weeping of the earth for what is lost.

By evening, when confirmation of these thoughts seems again withheld, I think of going back upriver, or up some other river than this one, to begin again.

I will tell you something. It is to the thought of the river's banks that I most frequently return, their wordless emergence at a headwaters, the control they urge on the direction of the river, mile after mile, and their disappearance here on the beach as the river enters the ocean. It occurs to me that at the very end the river is suddenly abandoned, that just before it's finished the edges disappear completely, that in this moment a whole life is revealed.

It is possible I am wrong. It is impossible to speak with certainty about very much.

It will not rain for the rest of the day. Lie down here and sleep. When you awake you will feel the pull of warm winds and wish to be gone. I will be standing somewhere on the beach staring at the breakers or the pirouettes of sanderlings, meditating on the distant murmuring of whales; but I can as easily turn inland, go upriver, and begin again.

When you awake, if you follow the river into the trees I will be somewhere ahead or beyond, like a flight of crows. When you are suddenly overwhelmed with a compassion that staggers you and you begin to run along the bank, at a moment when your fingers brush the soft skin of a deer-head orchid and you see sun-drenched bears stretching in an open field like young men, you will know a loss of guile and that the journey has begun.

The Search for the Heron

I SEE YOU ON THE FAR SIDE OF THE RIVER, STANDING at the edge of familiar shadows, before a terrified chorus of young alders on the bank. I do not think you know it is raining. You are oblivious to the *thuck* of drops rolling off the tube of your neck and the slope of your back. (Above, in the sweepy cedars, drops pool at the tips of leather needles, break away, are sheered by the breeze, and, *thuck*, hit the hollow-boned, crimson-colored shoulders of the bird and fall swooning into the river.)

Perhaps you know it is raining. The intensity of your stare is then not oblivion, only an effort to spot between the rain splashes in the river (past your feet, so well-known, there beneath the hammered surface like twigs in the pebbles) the movement of trout.

I know: your way is to be inscrutable. When pressed you leave. This is no more unexpected or mysterious than that you give birth to shadows. Or silence. I watch from a distance. With respect. I think of standing beside you when you have died of your own brooding over the water—as shaken as I would be at the collapse of a cathedral, wincing deep inside as at the screech of an overloaded cart.

You carry attribution well, refusing to speak. With your warrior's feathers downsloped at the back of your head, those white sheaves formed like a shield overlaying your breast, your gray-blue cast, the dark tail feathers—do you wear wolves' tails about your ankles and dance in clearings in the woods when your blood is running? I wonder where you have fought warrior. Where!

You retreat beneath your cowl, spread wings, rise, drift upriver as silent as winter trees.

I follow you. You have caught me with your reticence. I will listen to whatever they say about you, what anyone who has seen you wishes to offer—and I will return to call across the river to you, to confirm or deny. If you will not speak I will have to consider making you up.

Your sigh, I am told, is like the sound of rain driven against tower bells. You smell like wild ginger. When you lift your foot from the river, water doesn't run off it to spoil the transparent surface of the shallows. The water hesitates to offend you. You stare down with that great yellow eye, I am told, like some prehistoric rattlesnake: that dangerous, that blinding in your strike, that hate-ridden. But (someone else has insisted) you really do smell like wild ginger, and snakes smell like cucumbers. A false lead.

Cottonwoods along the river, stained with your white excrement, are young enough to volunteer complaint about you. They have grown so fast and so high with such little effort that they can understand neither failure nor triumph. So they will say anything they think might be to their advantage. I, after a somewhat more difficult life, am aware that they will lie, and that lies serve in their way.

(It was one of these who told me you were without mercy and snakelike.) One of them said something about your fishy breath—vulgar talk, I know. But I heard it out. It is, after all, in their branches where you have dreamed at night, as immobile as a piece of lumber left in their limbs, and considered your interior life. This idea attracts me. I know: this is not something to inquire into with impunity, but I did not start out on this to

please you. And in spite of my impatience I am respect-
ful.

One dream alone reveals your grief. The trees said
you dreamed most often of the wind. You dreamed that
you lived somewhere with the wind, with the wind rippling your feathers; and that children were born of this,
that they are the movement of water in all the rivers.
You wade, it is suggested, among your children, staring
hard, pecking in that lightning way your life from the
water that is your child; and sleeping in trees that do
not hold you sacred.

I know why you appear so fierce and self-contained.
I can imagine fear in the form of a frog in your beak
screaming and you, undisturbed, cool. When you finally
speak up, feigning ignorance with me won't do; enig-
matic locutions, distracting stories of the origin of the
universe—these will not do. I expect the wisdom of the
desert out of you.

The cottonwoods also told me of a dance, that you
dreamed of a dance: more than a hundred great blue
herons riveted by the light of dawn, standing with wind-
riffled feathers on broad slabs of speckled gray granite,
river-washed bedrock, in that sharp, etching backlight,
their sleek bills glinting, beginning to lift their feet from
the thin sheet of water and to put them back down. The
sound of the rhythmic splash, the delicate *kersplash* of
hundreds of feet, came up in the sound of the river and
so at first was lost; but the shards of water, caught blinding in the cutting light (now the voices, rising, a keening)
began to form a mist in which appeared rainbows against
the white soft breasts; and where drops of water dol-
loped like beads of mercury on the blue-gray feathers,
small rainbows of light here, and in the eyes (as the
voices, louder, gathering on one, high, trembling note)
rainbows—the birds cradled in light shattered in rainbows everywhere, and with your great blue wings fan-
ning that brilliant mist, open, utterly vulnerable and
stunning, you urged them to begin to revolve in the light,

stretching their wings, and you lay back your head and closed the steely eyes and from deep within your belly came the roar of a cataract, like the howling of wolves—that long moment of your mournful voice. The birds quieted, their voices quieted. The water quieted, it quieted, until there was only your quivering voice, the sound of the birth of rivers, tapering finally to silence, to the sound of dawn, the birds standing there full of grace. One or two feathers floating on the water.

I understand it is insensitive to inquire further, but you see now your silence becomes even more haunting.

I believe we will dance together someday. Before then will I have to have been a trout, bear scars from your stabbing misses and so have some deeper knowledge? Then will we dance? I cannot believe it is so far between knowing what must be done and doing it.

The cottonwoods, these too-young trees, said once, long ago, you had a premonition in a nightmare. An enormous owl arrived while you slept and took your daughter away, pinioned in his gray fists. You woke, bolt upright, in the middle of the night to find her there, undisturbed beside you. You aired your feathers, glared into the moon-stilled space over the water and went uneasily back to sleep. In the morning—your first glance—the limb was empty. You were young, you had also lost a wife, and you went down to the river and tore out your feathers and wept. The soundlessness of it was what you could not get over.

The cottonwoods said there was more, but I put up my hand, tired, on edge at the sound of my own voice asking questions. I went into the trees, wishing to cry, I thought, for what had been lost, feeling how little I knew, how anxious I was, how young.

The big maples, where you have slept since then—I resolved to ask them about your dreams. No; they refused. I climbed up in their limbs, imploring. They were silent. I was angered and made a fool of myself beating

on the trunks with my fists screaming, "Tell me about
the bird! It is only a bird!"

Learning your dreams unnerved me. What unholy
trespass I had made.

When I regained my composure I apologized, touching the maple trunks gently with my fingers. As I departed a wind moved the leaves of a low branch against
my face and I was embarrassed, for I was waiting for
some sign of understanding. I walked on, alert now to
the wind showing here and there in the grass. The wind
suddenly spoke of you as of a father. The thoughts were
incomplete, hinting at something incomprehensible, un-
graspable, but I learned this: you are able to stand in
the river in such a way that the wind makes no sound
against you. You arrange yourself so that you cast no
shadow and you stop breathing for half an hour. The
only sound is the faint movement of your blood. You
are quiet enough to hear fish swimming toward you.

When I asked, discretely, whether long ago you might
have fought someone, some enemy whose name I might
recognize, the wind was suddenly no longer there. From
such strength as is in you I suspect an enemy. I have
inquired of the stones at the bottom of the river; I have
inquired of your other enemy, the pine marten; I
have waded silently with your relatives, the bitterns, alert
for any remarks, all to no avail.

I have been crippled by my age, by what I have known,
as well as by my youth, by what I have yet to learn, in
all these inquiries. It has taken me years, which might
have been spent (by someone else) seeking something
greater, in some other place. I have sought only you.
Enough. I wish to know you, and you will not speak.

It is not easy to tell the rest, but I know you have
heard it from others. Now I wish you to hear it from
me. I took bits of bone from fish you had eaten and
pierced my fingers, letting the blood trail away in the
current. I slept on what feathers of yours I could find.

From a tree felled in a storm I took your nest, climbed with it to a clearing above the river where there was a good view, as much sky as I could comprehend. Bear grass, pentstemon, blue gilia, wild strawberries, Indian paintbrush growing there. Each night for four nights I made a small fire with sticks from the old nest and looked out toward the edge of the shadows it threw. On the last night I had a great dream. You were standing on a desert plain. You were painted blue and you wore a necklace of white salmon vertebrae. Your eyes huge, red. Before you on the dry, gray earth a snake coiled, slowly weaving the air with his head. You spoke about the beginning of the world, that there was going to be no fear in the world, that everything that was afraid would live poorly.

The snake said coldly, weaving, yes, there would be fear, that fear would make everything strong, and lashed out, opening a wound in your shoulder. As fast, you pinned his head to the ground and said—the calmness in your voice—fear might come, and it could make people strong, but it would be worth nothing without compassion. And you released the snake.

I awoke sprawled in bear grass. It was darker than I could ever remember a night being. I felt the spot on the planet where I lay, turned away from the sun. My legs ached. I knew how old I was lying there on the top of the mountain, a fist of cold air against my breast as some animal, a mouse perhaps, moved suddenly under my back.

An unpronounceable forgiveness swept over me. I knew how much had to be given away, how little could ever be asked. The sound of geese overhead in the darkness just then, and all that it meant, was enough.

I leap into the jade color of the winter river. I fight the current to reach the rocks, climb up on them and listen for the sound of your voice. I stand dripping, shivering in my white nakedness, in the thin dawn light. Waiting. Silent. You begin to appear at a downriver bend.

THE LOG JAM

1946

IN SEPTEMBER, WHEN BEARBERRY LEAVES WERE ready to pick, after the first storm had come upvalley like a drunken miner headed home, snapping limbs as thick as your arms off the maples, Olin Sanders caught a big tree barberchairing and was dead before they could get him out of the woods. They laid him across the laps of two men in the back of the truck and sent word ahead. When they got down to the road his wife was there crying, with pink curlers like pine cones in her hair and in black knit slacks too small for her stout legs and a loose hanging white blouse. And two county sheriffs, drawn by the word of death, wearing clean, pressed clothing, like clerks. When she looked in through the window of the truck and saw him broken in half like a buckled tin can she raised her fists to beat at the thing responsible and began beating the truck. When the sheriff held her back and said in a polite voice, "Now, control yourself," she began beating her thighs. One of the men stepped up and punched the sheriff.

All this time the son, in whose lap the father's broken head was cradled, sat silent. He was aware of the beginning of something else, more than his father's end. His pants were wet with his father's blood.

That night the boy left the house, walked past his father's shirts hanging to dry on the line, and drove up the Warner Creek Road to the place where they had been cutting. He sidestepped downslope with the chain-saw in his hands to reach the stump of the tree (the blood congealed like dark sap on the wood) and cut it off, cut off the top of the stump with the stain of his father's death on it, the saw screaming in the dim night. With a choker and a length of cable he hauled the butt round uphill and cursed and jacked it into the back of his pickup.

He came off Warner Mountain to the Granite Creek Road and went down Granite Creek until he came to the equipment shed, where a logging bridge crossed the river to the highway side. With a front loader and a length of chain he yanked the slab of wood out of the pickup, drove out onto the bridge and with jerking motions and the hiss of hydraulics he twisted the machine crosswise, tipped the bucket and dumped the slab of fir into the river.

He put the front loader away and drove home.

No one had ever done anything like this before. The lack of any tradition in it bothered the boy. As he walked past the trees near the house he was suddenly afraid. His mother was awake, sitting in the darkened living room when he walked in, wearing the tattered quilt robe that embarrassed him when his friends were around. Behind the glow of her cigarette she asked where he had been.

The butt round came back to the surface of the river, the thunderous sound of its plunge evaporating in the night, and it moved off like a dark iceberg riding low in the water. A few miles and it beached quietly on the cobbles of an island.

1951

Cawley Besson and his family—a wife called June, two boys, and a mixed-breed dog—came to work for the Forest Service. There was timber then, timber uncruised

in backcountry valleys. Douglas firs ten feet through at
the base and straight-grained for two hundred and fifty
feet. Dense, slow-grown wood. It was show-off timber
and no need to spare it.

Cawley opened roads to it. He was tight-bellied, ded-
icated, and clipped in his manners. He left early for work
and came home late, with a reputation, he said, to think
about. He had places to go after this job he told his wife
(lying next to him, listening to him, wondering when
they would make love again), places to go.

On a hot Sunday in June, Cawley sat at the river's
edge in a pair of shorts, eating a picnic lunch, thinking
about Monday, drinking cold beer and watching his
sons. The boys were throwing rocks into the river, which
the dog chased until he felt the current at his legs and
stepped back. Cawley liked the feel of this: he looked
toward his wife, feeling the warmth of his own body.
The boy swept past him, gesticulating silently, before
the scream arrived in his ears, as the dog ran over him
barking, and he looked to see the other son standing
motionless at the river's edge with his hands over his
mouth.

Cawley leaped to his feet, spilling food away, calling
out, running to catch up, cursing jibberish. He could
not swim, the boy either. He saw the small white face in
the dark water, the sunlight bright in his short wet hair,
and what lay ahead began to close in on him. The boy,
wide-eyed and quiet, went with the river.

Cawley continued to run. The panic got into him like
leeches. The beer was coming up acid in his mouth. The
river bore the boy on and he calculated how fast, running harder to get ahead, yelling to the boy Hold on!
Hold on! Jesus hold on. A little ahead now. He saw the
vine maple coming at him, grabbed it, bent it, broke it
so fast he felt hope, ran hard into the shallows ahead of
the boy to throw the end of the long branch to him—
who spun off its tip with his hands splayed, rigid. Cawley
dropped the limb and churning high-legged and mad,

chest deep and with a sudden plunge had the boy, had
his shirt, and was flailing for shore, grabbing for rocks
in the river bed that swept by under him. His feet
touched ground and held. His fist was white with his
grip twisted in the boy's tee-shirt—the boy could hardly
breathe against his clutch.

The maple limb drifted downriver and came to rest
among willows, near a log round on which dark stains
were still visible.

1954

A storm came this year, against which all other storms
were to be measured, on a Saturday in October, a balmy
afternoon. Men in the woods cutting firewood for winter, and children outside with melancholy thoughts
lodged somewhere in the memory of summer. It built
as it came up the valley as did every fall storm, but the
steel-gray thunderheads, the first sign of it anyone saw,
were higher, much higher, too high. In the stillness before it hit, men looked at each other as though a fast
and wiry man had pulled a knife in a bar. They felt the
trees falling before they heard the wind, and they
dropped tools and scrambled to get out. The wind came
up suddenly and like a scythe, like piranha after them,
like seawater through a breach in a dike. The first blow
bent trees half to the ground, the second caught them
and snapped them like kindling, sending limbs raining
down and twenty-foot splinters hurtling through the air
like mortar shells to stick quivering in the ground. Bawl-
ing cattle running the fences, a loose lawnmower bump-
ing across a lawn, a stray dog lunging for a child racing
by. The big trees went down screaming, ripping open
holes in the wind that were filled with the broken-china
explosion of a house and the yawing screech of a pickup
rubbed across asphalt, the rivet popping and twang of
phone and electric wires.

It was over in three or four minutes. The eerie, sucking silence it left behind seemed palpably evil, something that would get into the standing timber, like insects, a memory.

No one was killed. Roads were cut off, a bridge buckled. No power. A few had to walk in from places far off in the steep wooded country, arriving home later than they'd ever been up. Some said it pulled the community together, others how they hated living in the trees with no light. No warning. The next day it rained and the woods smelled like ashes. It was four or five days before they got the roads opened and the phones working, electricity back. Three sent down to the hospital in Holterville. Among the dead, Cawley Besson's dog. And two deer, butchered and passed quietly in parts among neighbors.

Of the trees that fell into the river, a number came up like beached whales among willows at the tip of an island.

1957

Rebecca Grayson drove forty-one miles each morning to work in a men's clothing store in town and came back each evening in time to fix her husband's dinner. It was a job that had paid for births and funerals, for weddings and a second automobile but it left her depressed and stranded now, at fifty-six, as if it were a clear defeat, invisible but keenly known to her.

Her husband operated a gas station and logging supply shop in Beaver Creek, a small town on the river. They had had four daughters, which had caused Clarence Grayson a kind of dismay from which he never recovered. It wasn't a country for raising daughters, he thought. He lived as though he were waiting for wounds to heal before moving on.

He hardly noticed, when she helped him in the shop

on Saturdays, that someone often came by with wild-
flowers for her, or to tell a story, to ask had she seen
the skunk cabbage in Danmeier's field or the pussy willows blooming, sure signs of spring. Clarence appreci-
ated these acts of kindness, while he finished a job for
whoever it was, as a duty done that he had no way with.

Men were attracted to Rebecca in an innocent but
almost hungry way, as though needing the pleasure she
took in them. Because there was never a hint of anything
but friendship, their attentions both pleased her and left
her with a deep longing, out of which, unashamed, she
lay awake at night in a self-embrace of fantasy.

Late at night, when he couldn't sleep, Clarence would
roll over to her and try to speak. Sometimes he would
begin to cry and sob in anger at a loss he couldn't find
the words for. He cried against her negligee and drove
his fist weakly into his pillow. On those nights she held
him until the pain ran its course, and said nothing of
her own yearning.

After the last daughter had married she thought they
could go away. In a deeply private place she wished to
go to Europe, alone; but she could not bear the thought
of his loneliness and did not believe that in a journey
together there could be any joy.

One summer evening while Clarence was in the living
room reading, she sat on their bed with her face lowered
to a glass bowl of dried blossoms in her lap, a pool of
musky odor that triggered memory and passion in her
and to which she would touch her face in moments when
she needed friendship. Twenty years of anniversary
roses, flowers from her first gardens, wildflowers from
men who were charmed by her, a daughter's wedding
bouquet. She felt the tears run the length of her nose
and the tightness of her small fists pressing against her
knees. She wished to be rid of it, and she rose with the
bowl and left.

In the dark yard by the side of the house she took off
her dress and her soft underclothes. With the bowl

firmly in her grip she walked down to the river and stepped in. The cold water rose against her as she moved away from the shore, lapped at her pale belly, and she felt a resolve as strong as any love she could ever remember. Her breasts hardened in the cold air. Waist deep in the water, her feet bent painfully around the stones (on the far bank she could see into the living rooms of people she knew), she scattered the first handful on the water. The pieces landed soundlessly and teetered quickly away. She flung the dry petals, the shrunken blossoms and the discolored flakes until the bowl was empty, and then dipped its lip to the current to swirl it clean.

She stood there, numb to the cold, until the wind had dissipated the perfume, listening to the wash around her hips, feeling the excitement of something she could not grasp. She thought of herself going on, like the river, without a break, with two herons flying overhead, untouchable and graceful, toward an undetermined destination. She had no wish to explain the feeling to anyone.

Of the flowers she threw on the water, some floated down as far as the log jam and hung up in its crevices.

1964

By this time beaver had come back to the valley, once having been trapped out. They were few and save for the sight of alders cut along the creeks their lives went unnoticed. One of the dams blocked a feeder stream above Bear Creek and was found one morning in the fall by a boy hunting deer. He walked across, testing it idly as he went, then throwing his weight to it, trying to make it spring. He came to a halt and surveyed the dam with surprise, for it did not give. On the far side he set his gun against a tree and cut an alder pole, stripping the leaves and sharpening the point with swift, deft

strokes of his knife. Walking back across the span he
began to probe the structure, looking for an opening
with depth. He found such a place and twisting the pole
into it began to pry and root with the tip, seeking better
leverage. Bracing his legs and putting all the strength
of his back and upper arms into it, he broke out a wedge
of mud and twigs. Against this breach he began to use
the pole like a post-hole digger, raising it above his head
and ramming deeper and deeper, prying against any
purchase. The green twigs were supple and difficult to
break so he turned to the knife. Cut through, then pry.
He was beginning to sweat. As he took off his jacket he
saw the beaver surface in the middle of the pond. He
hunkered quietly off the dam and hid in the brush. The
beaver, motionless in the center of departing concentric
rings of water, followed each movement.

The boy stared at the beaver, angry for having allowed
himself to be seen. He could feel his heart pounding,
the sudden compression of his muscles, smell his own
warm odors. His hand located a rock. In one fluid mo-
tion he rose to fire it with tremendous strength, so hard
the hair jumped on his head with the snap of his body.
He missed. The beaver slipped under. He picked up
another rock. *Twoosh*. The sound of the stone cutting
into the pond steadied him. *Twoosh. Twoosh*.

He returned to the dam, to the place where he had
gouged an opening. Prying, batting, cutting, and kick-
ing; finally, against a fulcrum of boulders carried from
the shore, he broke through the mesh of limbs. He
stepped aside, disheveled. As the water flowed cleanly
through the cut he came to realize the break was too
shallow, only several inches below the surface of the
pond; and that it was too late in the day to go hunting.
And that the beaver had not shown himself again. He
cursed the beaver, threw the pry pole into the pond and,
taking his gun, walked off sullenly.

The pond drained to the level of the cut. After dark

the beaver came to the breach and began to weave a closure.

The boy threatened to return to the valley and trap beaver that winter but did not.

Alder branches from the dam were swept down Bear Creek and into the river, where they wedged in the log jam.

1973

The fir that grew next to the Thompsons' house was, by a count of its rings, 447 years old when it fell at dusk on a March day during dinner. Before it fell the sounds outside were only those of the river coming up softly through the trees and the calls of grosbeaks. Gene Thompson was able to hear other things as he sat at the table. He could hear trees growing and dying. (When he walked in the woods he could distinguish between the creaking of cedar and the creaking of hemlock, between the teeter of rocks in a stream and the heartbeat of a spotted owl. He lay in the woods with his ear pressed to the damp earth listening to the slow burrowing of tree roots, which he distinguished from the digging of moles or worms, or the sound of rivers moving deep in the earth.) When he listened with his forehead against a tree he heard the thinking of woodpeckers asleep inside. He heard the flow of sap which sounded like stratospheric winds to him.

Gene sat quietly at dinner listening to the fir by the house. He heard the sudden spread of a filigree of cracks in the termite-ridden roots, the groaning of fibers stretched as the tree shifted its weight, seventy tons, toward the river and a muffled popping in the earth as it gave way. He heard (the fork poised before his mouth) the sweeping brush of trailing limbs high overhead as it began its descent. With the first loud crack, the terrible whining screech of separation, the gasping, sucking noise in its wake as the tree sailed down, everyone looked up. The tree struck the earth like a sheet of iron and dinner leaped from the table. A soft after-rain of twigs.

Gene went out the door with his father.

"Holy cow!" he said, striding toward it.

It had taken other trees with it, broken the highway and lay with its top in the river. It had to be removed, said his father, right away, to let traffic through. "Six or seven feet," he said to an approaching neighbor, "through the butt and clean for two hundred feet." Lucky no one had been killed, he said. He knew its value. Prime old growth. Overmature. Cut right it could be worth $3,000. He figured it roughly, climbed up on it and paced off a measurement in the falling light while another son jerked a chain saw to life to begin to clear the road.

The boy squatted at the stump with his hands spread wide in the tawny sap. He had heard the slow movement of air through the lengthening termite tunnels and had known. He raised his hands from the stump and the sap hung stiffly from his fingers like spirals of honey.

The crown of the tree eventually washed downriver and became entangled at the tip of the island. In the years that followed a pair of osprey came and built a nest, and lived as well as could be expected in that country.

THE BEND

IN THE EVENINGS I WALK DOWN AND STAND IN THE trees, in light paused just so in the leaves, as if the change in the river here were not simply known to me but apprehended. It did not start out this way; I began with the worst sort of ignorance, the grossest inquiries. Now I ask very little. I observe the swift movement of water through the nation of fish at my feet. I wonder privately if there are for them, as there are for me, moments of faith.

The river comes around from the southeast to the east at this point: a clean shift of direction, water deep and fast on the outside of the curve, flowing slower over the lip of a broad gravel bar on the inside, continuing into a field of shattered boulders to the west.

I kneel and slip my hands like frogs beneath the surface of the water. I feel the wearing away of the outer edge, the exposure of rootlets, the undermining. I imagine eyes in the tips of my fingers, like the eyestalks of crayfish. Fish stare at my fingertips and bolt into the river's darkness. I withdraw my hands, conscious of the trespass. The thought that I might be observed disturbs me.

I've wanted to take the measure of this turn in the river, grasp it for private reasons. I feel closer to it now. I know which deer drink at which spots on this bank. I know of the small screech owl nesting opposite (I would point him out to you by throwing a stone in that direction but the gesture would not be appropriate.) I am familiar with the raccoon and fisher whose tracks appear here, can even tell them apart in the dark by delicately fingering the rim of their prints in the soil. I can hear the preparations of muskrats. On cold, damp nights I am aware of the fog of birds' breath that rolls oceanic through the trees above. Out there, I know which rocks are gripped by slumbering water striders, and where beneath the water lie the slipcase homes of caddis fly larvae.

I feel I am coming closer to it.

For myself, each day more of me slips away. Absorbed in seeing how the water comes through the bend, just so, I am myself, sliding off.

The attempt to wrestle meaning from this spot began poorly, with illness. A pain, slow in coming like so many, that seemed centered in the back of my neck. Then an acute yearning, as strong as the wish to be loved, pain along the ribs, and my legs started to give way. I awoke in the morning with my hands over my face as though astonished by my own dreams. As the weeks went on I moved about less and less, until finally I went to bed and lay there like summer leaves. I could hear the rain in the woods in the afternoon; the sound of the river, like the laughing of horses; smell faintly through the open window the breath of bears. Between these points I was contained, closed off like a spider by the design of a web. I tried to imagine that I was well, but the points of my imagination impaled me, and then a sense of betrayal emptied me.

I began to think (as on a staircase descending to an unexamined basement) about the turn in the river. If I could understand this smoothly done change of direction I could imitate it, I reasoned, just as a man puts what he reads in a story to use, substituting one point for another as he needs.

Several things might be measured I speculated: the
rate of flow of the water, the erosion of the outer bank,
the slope of the adjacent mountains, the changing radius
of curvature as the river turned west. It could be revealed neatly, affirmed with graphic authority.

I became obsessed with its calculation. I lay the plan
out first in my head, without recourse to paper. The
curve required calculus, and so some loss of accuracy;
and the precise depth of the river changed from moment to moment, as did its width. But I could abide this
for the promise of insight into my life.

I called on surveyors, geodesic scientists, hydrologists.
It was the work of half a year. It involved them in the
arduous toting of instruments back and forth across the
river and in tedious calculation. I asked that exacting
journals be kept, that no scrap of description be lost.
There were arguments, of course. I required that ren-
derings be done again, over and over. I became con-
vinced that in this wealth of detail a fixed reason for the
river's graceful turn would inevitably be revealed.

The workmen, defeated by the precision required, in
an anger all their own, hurled their theodolites into the
trees. (The repair of these instruments consumed more
time.) I understood that fights broke out. But I saw none
of this. I lay alone in the room and those in my employ
came and went politely with their notes. I knew they
thought it pointless, but there was their own employ-
ment to be considered, and they said the wage was fair.

Finally they reduced the bend in the river to an elegant
series of equations, and the books containing them and
a bewildering list of variables were all gathered together
and brought to my room. I had them placed on the
floor, stacked in a corner. I suddenly had the strength
for the first time, staring at this pile, to move, but I was
afraid. I put it off until morning; I felt my recovery was
certain, believed even more forcefully now that my own
resolution was at hand by an incontestable analogy.

That night I awoke to hear the dripping of water.

From the direction of the pile of notes came the sound of mergansers, the explosive sound they make when they are surprised on the water and suddenly fly off.

I lay back.

Moss grew eventually on the books. They began after a while to harden, to resemble the gray boulders in the river. Years passed. I smelled cottonwood on spring afternoons, and would imagine sunshine crinkling on the surface of the water.

In winter the windows remained open because I could not reach them.

One morning, without warning, I came to a dead space in my depression, a sudden horizontal view, which I seized. I pried myself from the room, coming down the stairs slow step by slow step, all the while calling out. Bears heard me (or were already waiting at the door). I told them I needed to be near the river. They carried me through the trees (growling, for they are not used to working together), throwing their shoulders to the alders until we stood at the outer bank.

Then they departed, leaving the odor of bruised grass and cracked bone hanging in the air.

The first thing I did was to feel, raccoonlike, with the tips of my fingers the soil of the bank just below the water's edge. I listened for the sound of water on the outer bar. I observed the hunt of the caddis fly.

I am now taking the measure of the bend in these experiences.

I have lost, as I have said, some sense of myself. I no longer require as much. And though I am hopeful of recovery, an adjustment as smooth as the way the river lies against the earth at this point, this is no longer the issue with me. I am more interested in this: from above, to a hawk, the bend must appear only natural and I for the moment inseparably a part, like salmon or a flower. I cannot say well enough how this single perception has dismantled my loneliness.

THE FALLS

SOMEONE MUST SEE TO IT THAT THIS STORY IS TOLD: you shouldn't think this man just threw his life away.

When he was a boy there was nothing about him to remember. He looked like anything else—like the trees, like other people, like his dog. The dog was part coyote. Sometimes he would change places with his dog. For a week at a time he was the dog and the dog was himself, and it went by unnoticed. It was harder on the dog, but the boy encouraged him and he did well at it. The dog's name was Leaves.

When the boy went to sleep in the hills he would become the wind or a bird flying overhead. It was, again, harder on the dog, running to keep up, but the dog knew the boy would be a man someday and would no longer want to be a bird or the wind, or even a half-breed dog like himself, but himself. Above all, the dog trusted in time.

This is what happened. The boy grew. Visions came to him. He began to see things. When he was eighteen he dreamed he should go up in the Crazy Mountains north of Big Timber to dream, and he went. He was careful from whom he took rides. Old cars. Old men only. He was old enough to be careful but not to know why.

The dreaming was four days. I do not know what came to him. He told no one. He spoke with no one. While he was up there the dog, Leaves, slept out on some rocks in the Sweetgrass River, where he would not be bothered, and fasted. I came at dawn and then at dusk to look. I could not tell from a distance if he was asleep or dead. Or about the dog. I would only know it was all right because each morning he was in a different position. The fourth morning—I remember this one the best, the sun like fire on the October trees, so many spider webs sunken under the load of dew, the wind in them, as though the trees were breathing—he was gone. I swam out to see about the dog. Wild iris petals there on the green moss. That was a good dog.

The man was back home in two days. He washed in the river near his home.

He got a job down there around Beatty and I didn't see him for two or three years. The next time was in winter. It was the coldest one I had ever been in. Chickadees froze. The river froze all the way across. I never saw that before. I picked him up hitchhiking north. He had on dark cotton pants and a light jacket and lace shoes. With a brown canvas bag and a hat pulled down over his ears and his hands in his pockets. I pulled over right away. He looked sorry as hell.

I took him all the way up north, to my place. He had some antelope meat with him and we ate good. That was the best meat I ever had. We talked. He wanted to know what I was doing for work. I was cutting wood. He was going to go up to British Columbia, Nanaimo, in there, in spring to look for work. That night when we were going to bed I saw his back in the kerosene light. The muscles looked like water coming over his shoulders and going into the bed of his spine. I went over and hugged him.

I woke up the next morning when it was just getting light. I could not hear the sound of the river and the silence frightened me until I remembered. I heard chopping on the ice. I got dressed and went down. The earth was like rock that winter.

He had cut a hole a few feet across, black water boiling up, flowing out on the ice, freezing. He was standing in the hole naked with his head bowed and his arms straight up over his head with his hands open. He had cut his arms with a knife and the red blood was running down them, down his ribs, slowing in the cold, to the black water. I could see his body shaking, the muscles starting to go blue-gray over his bones, the color of the ice. He called out in a voice so strong I sat down as though his voice had hit me. I had never heard a cry like that, his arms down and his fists squeezed tight, his mouth, those large white teeth, his forehead knotted. The cry was like a bear, not a man sound, like something he was tearing away from inside himself.

The cry went up like a roar and fell away into a trickle, like creek water over rocks at the end of summer. He was bent over with his lips near the water. His fist opened. He put water to his lips four times, and washed the blood off. He leaped out of that hole like a salmon and ran off west, around the bend, gone into the trees, very high steps.

I went down to look at the blood on the gray-white ice.

He cut wood with me that winter. He worked hard. When the trillium bloomed and the varied thrushes came he went north.

I did not see him again for ten years. I was in North Dakota harvesting wheat, sleeping in the back of my truck (parked under cottonwoods for the cool air that ran down their trunks at night like water). One night I heard my name. He was by the tailgate.

"You got a good spot," he said.

"Yeah. That you?"

"Sure."

"How you doing?"

"Good. Talk in the morning."

He sounded tired, like he'd been riding all day.

Next morning someone left, too much drinking, and
he got that job, and so we worked three weeks together,
clear up into Saskatchewan, before we turned around
and drove home. When we came through Stanley Basin
in Idaho we crossed over a little bridge where the Salmon
River was only a foot deep, ten feet across. It came across
a big meadow, out of some quaking aspen. "Let's go up
there," he said. "I bet that's good water." We did. We
camped up in those aspen and that was good water. It
was sweet like a woman's lips when you are in love and
holding back.

We came home and he stayed with me that winter,
too. I was getting old then and it was good he was
around. In the spring he left. He told me a lot that
winter, but I can't say these things. When he spoke about
them it was like the breeze when you are asleep in the
woods: you listen hard, but it is not easy. It is not your
language. He lived in the desert near antelope one year,
by a lake where geese came in the spring. The antelope
taught him to run. The geese did not teach him anything, he said, but it was good to be around them. The
water in the lake was so clear when the geese floated
they seemed to be suspended, twenty or twenty-five feet
off the ground.

The morning he left the desert he took a knife and
carefully scraped his whole body. He put some of these
small pieces of skin in the water and scattered the rest
over the sagebrush.

He went to work then in another town in Nevada
somewhere, I forget, in a lumberyard and he was there
for a long time, five or six years. He took time off a lot,
went into the mountains for a few weeks, a place where
he could see the sun come up and go down. Clean out
everything bad that had built up.

When he left that place he went to Alaska, around
Anchorage somewhere, but couldn't find any work and
ended up at Sitka fishing and then went to Matanuska
Valley, working on a farm there. All that time he was

alone. Once he came down to see me but I was gone. I
knew it when I got home. I went down to the river and
saw the place where he went into the water. The ground
was soft around the rocks. I knew his feet. I am not a
man of great power, but I took what I had and gave it
to him that time, everything I had. "You keep going,"
I said. I raised my hands over my head and stepped into
the water and shouted it again, "You keep going!" My
heart was pounding like a waterfall.

That time after he left he was gone almost ten years
again. I had a dream he was living up on those salmon
rivers in the north. I don't know. Maybe it was a no-
account dream. I knew he never went south.

Last time I saw him he came to my house in the fall.
He came in quiet as air sitting in a canyon. We made
dinner early and at dusk he went out and I followed
him because I knew he wanted me to. He cut twigs from
the ash and cottonwood and alder and I got undressed.
He brushed my body with these bank-growing trees and
said I had always been a good friend. He said this was
his last time. We went swimming a little. There is a good
current at that place. It is hard to swim.

Later we went up to the house and ate. He told me a
story about an old woman who tried to keep two hus-
bands and stories about a man who couldn't sing but
went around making people pay to hear him sing anyway. I laughed until I was tired out and went to bed.

I woke up suddenly, at the end of a dream. It was the
same dream I had once before, about him climbing up
a waterfall out of the sky. I went to look in his bed. He
was gone. I got dressed and drove my truck to the falls
below the willow flats where I killed my first deer many
years ago. I ran into the trees, fighting the vine maple
and deadfalls, running now as hard as I could for the
river. The thunder of that falls was all around me and
the ground shaking. I came out on the river, slipping
on the black rocks glistening in the moonlight. I saw him
all at once standing at the lip of the falls. I began to

shiver in the damp cold, the mist stinging my face, moonlight on the water when I heard that bear-sounding cry
and he was shaking up there at the top of the falls, silver
like a salmon shaking, and that cry louder than the falls
for a moment, and then swallowed and he was in the
air, turning over and over, moonlight finding the silver-
white of his sides and dark green back before he cut
into the water, the sound lost in the roar.

I did not want to leave. Sunrise. I went up onto the
willow flats where I could see the sky. I felt the sunlight
going deep into my hair. Good fall day. Good day to go
look for chinquapin nuts, but I sat down and fell asleep.

When I awoke it was late. I went back to my truck
and drove home. On the way I was wondering if I felt
strong enough to eat salmon.

THE SHALLOWS

THE OVERALL IMPRESSION HERE, AS ONE SURVEYS the river spread out over the gravel bars, is of a suspension of light, as though light were reverberating on a membrane. And a loss of depth. The slope of the riverbed here is nearly level, so the movement of water slows; shallowness heightens the impression of transparency and a feeling for the texture of the highly polished stones just underwater. If you bring your eye to within a few inches of the surface, each stone appears to be submerged in glycerin yet still sharply etched, as if held closely under a strong magnifying glass in summer light. An illusion—that insight into the stone is possible, that all distraction can be peeled away or masked off, as in preparation for surgery, while sunlight penetrates and highlights—is encouraged.

Beyond the light, a loss of depth, as the subsurface nears the surface, as though the river were exposing itself to examination. Kneel with your ear to the water; beyond the *plorp* of it in a hollow and the slooshing gurgle through labyrinthine gravels, are the more distant sound of its fugue. A musical notebook lies open— alto and soprano clefs, notes tied and trills, turned notes, indications of arpeggio and glissando. Plunge your ear in suddenly—how it vanishes. Take the surface of the river between your thumb and forefinger. These textures are exquisite, unexpected.

Step back. The light falling on the dry rocks beneath
our feet seems leathery by comparison. And this is another difference: the light on the dry rock is direct,
shaftlike, almost brutal, so rigid one can imagine a sound
like crystal lightly stung with a fingernail if it were
touched; while the cooler light on the rocks in the water
is indirect, caressing. This is why if you pluck a stone
from the water and allow it to dry it seems to shrivel. It
is the same as that phenomenon where at dusk you are
able to see more clearly at the periphery of your vision.
An indirect approach, the sidelong glance of the sun
through the water, coaxes out the full character of the
naturally reticent stone.

Fish are most exposed in the shallows, and so move
through quickly. One afternoon I saw an osprey here,
reminiscent of a grizzly at the water's edge anticipating
salmon. A fish came by; he took off lightly and snatched
it from the water.

Here, step across; you'll be able to examine things
better out on the gravel bars. (We are fortunate for the
day—temperatures in the eighties I understand.) Look,
now at the variety of stones. Viewed from the bank these
gravel bars seem uniformly gray, but bend close and you
see this is not true. It's as though at first glance nothing
were given away. You could regard this as the stone's
effort to guard against intrusion by the insincere. Here,
look at these: the red, chert, a kind of quartz; this
streaked gray, basalt; the greenish one, a sedimentary
rock, shale, stained with copper; the blue—this is un-
common: chrysocolla, a silicate. The white, quartzite.
Obsidian. Black glass. This brown, andesite. It's reas-
suring to hear the names, but it's not so important to
remember them. It's more important to see that these
are pieces of the earth, reduced, ground down to an
essential statement, that in our lifetime they are irreduc-
ible. This is one of the differences between, say, stones
and flowers.

I used to throw a few stones out into the river—underhand with a flick of the wrist, like this.

It is relatively simple, in a place where the river slows like this, fans out over the gravel, to examine aspects of its life, to come to some understanding of its history. See, for example, where this detritus has caught in the rocks? Raccoon whisker. Hemlock twig. Dead bumblebee. Deer-head orchid. Maidenhair fern. These are dry willow leaves of some sort. There are so many willows, all of which can interbreed. Trying to hold each one to a name is like trying to give a name to each rill trickling over the bar here, and making it stick. Who is going to draw the lines? And yet it is done. Somewhere this leaf has a name, *Salix hookeriana, Salix lasiandra.*

Piece of robin's egg, perhaps after a raid by a long-tailed weasel. Chip of yew tree bark. Fireweed. Snail shell—made out of the same thing as your fingernail. Here, tap it—Or a rattlesnake's rattles. Roll it around in your hand. Imagine the clues in just this. Counting the rings would tell you something, but no one is sure what. Perhaps all that is recorded is the anguish of snails. Oh, this is rare: fox hairs. You can tell by the coloring. Some say it is the degree of taper, the shape. Up above someplace a fox crossed over. Or was killed by someone.

Behind the larger stones—let's walk up this way—hung up in their crevices is another kind of detritus entirely, a layer of understanding that becomes visible only under certain circumstances, often after a thunderstorm, for example, when the air has a sudden three-dimensional quality and it appears it might be slit open neatly and examined from the inside. What you see then, tethered to the rocks as though floating on the silken threads of spider webs adrift in the balmy air, are the sighs of sparrows passing overhead. The jubilation of wind-touched aspens. The persistence of crayfish, the tentative sipping of deer, who have stepped clear of the cover of trees, the circumspection of lone fish.

And there are still other revelations beyond these. You can imagine what might be learned in a place like this if one took the time. Think only of the odors, some single strand of which might be nipped between rocks, of wild-flowers (lupine, avalanche lily, the white blossoms of bunchberry, yellow balsamroot, crimson currant), of musk (needle-toothed weasel, sleek-furred mink, bright-eyed fisher, grizzly bear on his rump, eating the seed pods of dogtooth violet), of suncracked earth, the odor of granite. Just so, by these invisible extensions is the character of the river revealed, is there some clue to what goes unexamined.

If you lie out flat on the stones—it seems odd to try, I know—you will feel—here, that's it—the warmth of the sunlight emanating from the stones. Turn your head to the side, ear to rock, and you will hear the earth revolving on its axis and an adjustment of stones in the riverbed. The heartbeats of salmon roe. One day I heard the footsteps of someone miles away, following someone else.

If you look up into the sky, straight up, eight or ten miles, it is possible to imagine the atmospheric tides, oceans of air moving against the edge of space in an ebb and flow as dependent on the phases of the moon. I believe lying here on the gravel bars cannot be too dif-ferent from lying on your back on the bottom of the ocean. You can choose to take this view or not, with no fear of consequence. The tides go on, regardless.

Let's walk along the edge.

The fish this garter snake has just snatched is called a dace, a relative of the creek chub, a life more obscure than most. The snake is *Thamnophis couchi hydrophila*, a western species. You can take the naming as far as you want. Some of the most enjoyable things—the way the water folds itself around that rock and drops away—have no names.

You are beginning to shiver, but it's nothing to be alarmed over. The stones warmed you; you sensed you were nestled in the earth. When you stood up fear pooled in an exposed feeling around your back. This is what to leave the earth means. To stand up, which you see bears do on occasion. At the very heart of this act is the meaning of personal terror.

Along the very edge of these gravel bars are some of the earth's seams. A person with great courage and balance could slip between the water and the rock, the wet and the dry, and perhaps never come back. But I think it must take as much courage to stay.

I have stood for hours on these gravel bars. I have seen the constellations reflected in chips of obsidian glass. My hands have gone out to solitary willows in the darkness. Once I lay without moving for days until, mistaking me for driftwood, birds landed nearby and began speaking in murmurs of Pythagoras and winds that blew in the Himalayas.

I regretted throwing stones into the river.

THE RAPIDS

PLEASE. STAND BACK.

Could you tell me if there was any trace of the boat?

No. That is—please. No one knows.

Are the men all presumed dead?

The children. Jesus, these people must have had children.

I wonder if I could get a word with you.

The river is like hell here.

You mean—

Should cover them with a tarp.

I've lived here all my life.

Yes?

And each year it happens like this. If not here, then somewhere else.

I'll bet there were three of them in the boat when it hit the logs.

Yeah. I'd expect.

Seventeen people here since 1970.

Should shut it down. State should.

Excuse me, would you say the river, well, a violent river like this, exacts a toll?

What?

Do people pay a price to use this river?

Mister, if a tree fell on you, would you say the forest was taking a toll?

What I meant—

Someday you might drown. You want your wife to say he paid the price?

And when you least expect it too, bub, just like these fellows.

These guys sure as hell knew it was dangerous to go into these rapids.

Went in, nevertheless.

Paid for it too.

That's what I meant.

We ain't talking the same price.

Excuse me, sir, did you see the accident?

No.

Well could you tell me what you know about it?

You ought to write down Collier Rapids. That's what the name of the place is.

Would you—I wonder if there are any members of the family you could point out here.

Jesus, look at the water come through that chute.

How old is this man? Twenty-four? Twenty-five? What a waste. And look at the wedding ring. He's married.

You know I hate to see anyone die. There's no need.

If you try on this side it ain't so bad, but you try on the other side and you whittled your last stick.

Mister, there wasn't anybody here when it happened. If you want to figure it all out why don't you just walk over there and look. You could throw a locomotive in that hole and never find it again.

Excuse me, do you live around here?

No, I was driving by.

Could you step back please, sir?

This guy's trying to write a story by talking to people who ain't got no answers. You ought to get yourself a boat and get out there. That's all the answer you'll need.

There's no need to yell at me. People have drowned here. Someone said seventeen in the last few years. This is a terrible thing. It makes people very sad.

River's the one sad.

My Lord, look how white his hands are. Why don't they put a jacket over his face.

Officer, I believe one of these poor men was at Nesmith's station last night. In a pickup pulling a boat. Had a kind of collie dog with him.

You're looking for someone to explain a couple of dead men and what's left of a boat.

The boat? Where?

There, in the water.

People want to be informed.

About these dead people and a broken boat? What are they gonna learn?

You ought to tell them to stay away from what they don't understand. These guys went in to the wrong chute. Won't work when the water's this high.

You got to know what you're doing.

Look, tore his shoes off. And I just—oh my—I just bought my husband a pair of pants like that. I'm taking them right back.

Can you imagine what they thought when they knew they were wrong, how lonely it must have been?

Pardon me, did you know these people?

Me?

Yes.

No.

Well several people have drowned here in the last few years. I wonder if you've ever been involved in a rescue—I presume this is your home here.

Yes. My wife drowned here in 1947.

You were present?

We were fishing on those rocks up above. Current pulled our boat away and we were stuck. We couldn't swim, either of us. We tried to get back, jumping from rock to rock. We'd slip and get swept farther downriver each time. I'd grab a rock, she'd grab my foot. She was a small woman, no bigger than this. Pulled me by the hair, right out of the mouth of one of those chutes. We were trapped on a small rock and it got dark. We knew no one was going to come that far down in a boat. We lay there shivering all night. In the morning it seemed the water had dropped some. We decided to wait until the afternoon. We sat there holding hands. I wanted to try it alone, come back with help somehow. It came time and we hugged. I jumped in and I heard her jump in suddenly upstream of me. She had hold of me for a moment and then was gone. I reached shore. I never saw her again. I ran below, along the bank, calling her name. I looked for her for days.

I'm sorry to hear that.

Sometimes it happens that way.

But you went right on living here anyway?

Yes. It's easiest to live where you have an understanding.

Death? You understand death?

No. It's more about anger. About blame.

Well, it's a very moving story.

Yes. Well, I have to go. Good luck to you.

You know, I came up here to do a story about these drownings. Now I think I might write it up with another point of view, a different slant.

Yes. Yes, that might be good.

THE SALMON

THERE IS NEVER, HE REFLECTED, A MOMENT OF CERtainty, only the illusion. And as he worked among the rocks in the middle of the river he thought on this deeply, so deeply that had his movements not been automatic he would have fallen off the rocks and into the river and been borne away.

In the summer light, even with the coolness of the water welling up around him in the air, thinking was all he was capable of; and this distraction left him exhausted and unbalanced so that at the end of the day the physical exhaustion he felt was something he lowered himself into, as into a hot bath. He pondered gentleness often. And he tried to pry (hefting the stones, conscious of the resonance between the idea in his mind and the work of his hands) into mysteries which remained as implacable as the faces of the stones.

The work was easier in the summer; in winter he was afraid of floods. He was always damp, and he slipped more often on the rocks then. In winter, on the worst days, he lost track of himself, and his acts seemed ludicrous. In summer he would feel sunlight against his back as he bent crane-like to the glacial outwash, and he enjoyed the way the light warmed his latissimi dorsi; and when the wind blew so the light seemed to have weight, he imagined how he fit into the wind, as neatly as trout poised in a deep riffle.

His hands moved over the stones (over granite, mot-
tled gabbro and red loaves of basalt) with a predatory
finesse, flicking to rocks his eye had only that moment
left, grasping, throwing in motions as smooth as his bare
back under the light. He seemed as sure of himself as
a cougar in ambush.

Some things he was certain of: that anadromous fish
return from the ocean to spawn; that he could lift a
hundred-pound rock; that it was always cooler in the
evening.

At night he would sit on the porch and stare for hours
at the piles of his stones, and imagine from the skeleton
of the idea how he would proceed. There were technical
problems, matters of physics. There were aesthetic difficulties to overcome, principally of color and texture in
the materials he had to work with, but also the texture
and colors, some seasonal, of the trees—maple, ash, cedar, alder, and cottonwood—on the far bank which
formed a backdrop. There were anatomical details to be
mindful of, a problem not only of accuracy but of ver-
isimilitude which he felt must go to the heart of the act.
He would solve each in its turn.

Out of each evening of thought he derived the energy
to continue, to rise the next morning and, remembering
all he had considered, to go to work, for it was (he had
been told) an act of madness, and he wished above all
to be sensible.

The gravel bar lay like a fish in the river, headed
upstream, dark dorsal surface to the sun. Sticks of driftwood neatly enfolded on its center crest, like the col-
lapsed spines of a fin, the dark rocks looking like scales—
about it an unphraseable mood of impermanence born
of its daily alteration and of eternal waiting, of migratory
fish and resident stones.

He had cleared the driftwood away. He had built a
bulwark of timbers on the upstream end of the bar to
divert the force of high water until he was finished, the
one practical concession he had made, anchored it in

the river bed, into bedrock. And there were the steel rods welded into a lattice against which he worked. The stones he fitted as haphazardly as rip-rap except on the surface, where they were fitted to bind against each other, to hold a curve in two planes without mortar. From upriver and downriver (this, in itself, two years of work) he had gathered the stones and (another year) sorted them: green shales and yellow sandstones, red slates and shaded gray gneiss, blue azurite, purple quartzes and cloudy white calcites. For iridescence, for translucence, he had to rely on individual stones and pebbles, agates, jaspers, and opals, some of which he had carried from as far away as the river's mouth.

Because his brothers had found favor with his father and he had found none, he thought. As simple as that. And a wife who had gone crazy (the fish enter the river) not out of anything he'd done or she'd done but out of the weight of her family (and move upstream), out of their perversity and sourness, generations of mistakes in which she had been a sudden clear expression, for which they had hated her. They had been afraid to have children. She was now with her sister (come upstream), reabsorbed like spent oxygen in a calm beyond his reach, forgotten but for the ingot of her that lay in him. He believed in reciprocation (come upstream) and rebalance, that others suffered as grievously as he had. He was without calculation (to spawn) or guile. And obsessed.

One evening, mired in the swamp of his thought, he leaned against the steel framework in a moment of quivering trust, as if he would weep, out of a nameless despair, and he heard coming up through the steel bars, up out of the bedrock, the murmuring of the earth— and he saw a flight of mergansers going downriver like a sigh, smelled sunshine on a thousand stones, knew by looking how cold the water would be against his belly, and that he was near the heart of it.

* * *

The room where he slept was bare as a room in a deserted hotel, but did not seem empty to him, only spare and ordered. A single shelf of books, most on the natural history of the salmonids, and a diminutive writing table, its legs barely enough to support his work (he would muse) but enough. Here some evenings, but only when he felt calm (if he was disturbed it was agony), he would write about the difficulties with his father, and of the things that had fallen apart in his life like a chrysalis flaking in the wind. He would write until he found a point of balance—and then abandon the journal as though leaping from a small airplane. On other evenings he would write in a more orderly hand and at tremendous length, sometimes until dawn: on salmon, on the dependability of their migration from the sea, on the irrefutable evidence of it. In the years until now, during the worst times, he held this idea like a walnut in his fist, cherishing its permanence, its meaning. It is how he came to conceive the stone fish.

The winter of the fourth year it began to take a finished look. He worked through these cold months and into the spring at a measured pace, which gave daily evidence of progress in spite of the enormity of the task, and also had a salutary effect on his mind. He thought less of the accidents in his life, nothing (he reflected) more than the turning of the earth, and focused instead on the sacred order to which the salmon coming upstream to spawn and die was central.

The fish was sixteen paces in length, nine feet high at the dorsal fin, *Oncorhynchus nerka*, a male sockeye with the irregularities of rut—the hooked jaw, the bright red mantel—with the air of a sumo wrestler, as Japanese in color, in its singular purpose, as a Samurai. Balanced on its belly and with its caudal fin swept to one side it was caught poised in an explosive movement. The natural armorial form of its scales served to conceal much of the stonework, but he had been so careful in the choice of stones that success here had been almost inevitable. The unsettling reality, the feeling of life in it, was heightened by the perfect shading of color, the smooth, rain-slick flanks, and the fish's eyes of hand-polished lapis, the barely visible teeth of white quartz and the narrow view down a cavernous, dark throat.

In mid-September the salmon entered the mouth of the river, two hundred miles below, and by early October they were upon him, thousands of thousands of fish, so many that they forced each other out onto the banks where the river narrowed. The movement was frantic, primal. Each year he'd watched them come finally into the small feeder creeks where, with gaping wounds washed a cloudy white, they would lie on their sides to keep one gill submerged and so breathe, move on to a pool, spawn, spill their eggs in a tail-dug basin over which the males, gaunt with hunger, glassy-eyed, exploded their milt, the seminal discharge settling over the eggs like cirrus clouds. In a matter of days they died, from which detritus their children fed. It all left him stunned.

In this year it was no different. In mid-September, into water blue-green with the mineral drainage of glaciers, the salmon who had come down this same river as small fry bore off, headed up into its reaches again. They heaved through white water where a creek washed in, some turning off, each as keen of nose as it had to be. They ate nothing, hurled themselves off the river floor into the roar of falls and rapids where they were maimed and killed and some went over and continued, dreaming perhaps of the ocean fastness and of gentler currents.

In these final months he finished. What he had imagined over the years of evenings had been engineered and it stood before him as the thing he most trusted. In the days of waiting for the salmon, he achieved a level of serenity heightened beyond any he had known before. Under this calming influence he decided impulsively to study Japanese. The connection between the fish and the culture seemed to him both incongruous and appropriate. He could imagine salmon choosing to live in Japanese houses, which had about them something of the ocean, which seemed submerged. He could think of the fish writing in that apposite calligraphy, that if they left messages they would leave them in this form, and on rice tissue papers as delicate and strong as the walls of the house.

One evening in October when he had begun to worry that the fish would not come, a rain storm swept up the valley. The great stone fish glistened as though it had just at that moment burst forth. Walking out to it, he felt a fierce pride in its form, and he headed downriver with this idea. In the shallows after a few hundred yards—it was difficult to see but the rain-shattered surface of the river revealed it with a precision that startled him—were salmon, their dark glistening backs as far as he could see. For several moments it was not clear to him what they were doing, that they were slowly turning around. The rain, sweeping in wind-driven sheets, made a sound that sheltered him from panic, but his guts fell away from his heart. He turned to look upstream at the stone fish, one lapis eye glaring with its black shining obsidian pupil in the turned head, the jaw agape, and the monument struck him suddenly with the depth of his desperation—the pages of his journal, the words pounded out like this rain on his shoulders. Overwhelmed with an understanding of the assumption in his act, made the more grotesque by its perfection, he waded stupefied into the water where the fish maneuvered, milling, trying to turn around. He staggered amongst them, trying to form a statement of apology, putting his fingers to their dark backs until they were gone, until he realized that they were gone.

He brought his hands to his face and for a while, in the passing mist of the rainstorm, he imagined what they would say. That it was the presence of the stone fish that had offended them (he tried to grasp the irreverence of it, how hopelessly presumptuous it must have seemed), that it was an order born out of fear, understood even by salmon, to be discarded as quickly as nightmares so that life could go on.

When he stood beside the fish he realized for the first time how flawless it was, that the ravages of the upstream journey were nowhere revealed. He thought of dismantling it, but instead removed only the obsidian pupils from the lapis eyes, which he dropped without looking into the rushing water as he crossed to the opposite bank.

In later years he wrote poetry in a beautiful Japanese hand in which he balanced the stonework of Machu Picchu against the directionless flight of butterflies. In this manner he slowly reclaimed his own life.

HANNER'S STORY

THERE ARE THOSE WHO SAY THAT THINGS WERE once better in this valley, that many years ago there was a different kind of life. I have listened patiently to these stories. They are idyllic and farfetched. I believe they represent hopeful longing on the part of those who tell them, a wish for a more orderly life, a life, ultimately, less cruel to them. These stories—they are called Sheffield stories—are told principally by the older people, the life-long residents, and evangelically, as though to overcome and smother incipient suspicion in the listener. I go on listening, though there seems no chance now that they will supply the detail I wish to hear, because of the attitude they have taken.

There is a man called Hanner, a retired guide on the river, who worked in his youth in the woods (as have most men here), whose hands bear the marks of trouble with wire rope and fish line and knives, who appears to have given his life over to a trenchant bitterness. The roots of it may be older, but he has been visited late in life by every tragedy. His only son went to prison for a criminal act with a child. His wife died of leukemia, slowly and before he retired. Vandals have smashed the windshield of his pickup on different occasions and turned his horses loose. One of the horses, a roan mare he never rode, was struck and killed by a school bus. He is without family. He does little in a day but move from

115

one cafe to another drinking coffee and listening in
silence to the stories around him. Sometimes he tells
stories, about fishing. About outlanders he has guided
down the river. People consider him sour, self-absorbed,
and without wisdom. But he has lived here all his life
and they say he is sharp-eyed; and that cannot be overlooked by someone like myself, they have said, interested
in verifying a story.

Hearing all this, I would think to myself: he will not
lie.

When I first encountered Hanner he was standing at
a distance with his hands in the pockets of his khaki
trousers, silhouetted in the tunnel of his open barn
against a pale blue summer sky. I needed directions,
and in search of local knowledge had wandered much
farther onto his property than I wished. He seemed to
be doing nothing at all; with a sideward movement of
his head he gave me his attention as I approached. He
was detached though explicit in giving directions and I
went on to find my way without trouble.

I walked away from the barn that day consstricted in
the throat, believing that for all the disparagement Hanner gripped something remote and wild.

The next time we met I had occasion to pick him up
along the road. He would not have solicited a ride; his
pickup was out of service (I had seen it in town, at the
station) and as I saw him walking with a large brown
bag in his arms and slowed I recognized him and offered
him a ride. I dropped him off. He was cordial but did
not invite me to dinner. The third time I saw him was
in the evening. He was standing alone in the middle of
a one-lane logging bridge looking down at the river. I
do not, again, know what he was doing. Perhaps he
contemplated suicide. I stopped part way onto the
bridge. He turned; we regarded each other. It was clear
I was intruding, but as I moved off he stayed me with
his raised hands and said he would walk back with me.
I wondered that someone else had my habit of walking

in the dark, but asked him instead about the stories.

He sighed, as though caught in a great undertow, an obligation that meant a diversion from his purposes. But an obligation. His circumspect nature, I thought, would work in his favor as an arbiter of detail in such dreams as I had been hearing—if one indeed were interested in what had happened, as, to an extent, I was.

It was rubbish he told me, those stories of Sheffield. Told by disillusioned people (I raised my eyebrows in the darkness) who wanted to be more than they actually were, or to wound. He, himself, was bitter over events in his own life but (I could feel him shaking his head as we moved along the edge of the road beneath the trees) he did not delude himself. He lived within the moment of his life, harsh as it was, and blamed no one. He saw nothing but pining weakness in the Sheffield stories. They left you empty, he said, when you heard them, because they were full of a kind of hope that insulted life. They were disrespectful, he said.

The central history, from which the stories derive, is short. In 1841 an Illinois man called William Alder came into the valley and established a secular community like the one at New Harmony. The community was named Sheffield after the first family to have a child, a girl named Wilhelmina, and it prospered, due principally to a fortuitous location. There was rich alluvial soil in the river's floodplain, and there were open meadows between oak and ash islands in which to build and plant without the necessity of clearing timber. The hunting was good, the winter weather rainy but mild. (It was here, in sketching for me the original beauty of the area, that I heard the greatest embroidery and a wonderment in the voices.) But their fortune was still greater. On their very first visit to the ocean, only seventy miles farther west, they found a shipwreck, its hull intact and most of its stores dry and undisturbed. There was rock salt, copper sheathing, iron implements, calico cloth— it is hard to be sure what, precisely, was found, but they returned to the valley with all of it in several trips in one of the ship's lifeboats, in itself a good find.

There was a third factor that must be considered in the success of the community and though it is rarely emphasized it seems to me to be the most important. It had to do with the community's reception by the Quotaka. the native people of the region. They were a tall, Athabascan-speaking group described in the journals of Robert Gray, Donald McKenzie, and other early visitors as exceedingly hostile and treacherous. Among the Quotaka was a medicine man called Elishtanak. Incredibly, he was the physical twin in every aspect of William Alder. It seems the Quotaka must have looked on this favorably for they seemed to have indulged the settlers' presence immediately. It could just as well have been disastrous; they might have considered the uncanny resemblance blasphemous and killed every one of them. As it was, the Sheffield group and the Quotaka remained close. There were one or two intermarriages, though it seems no other formal bonds were ever avowed. (I am relying here principally on William Alder's journal.) After these intitial years of cooperative alliance, the Quotaka succumbed completely to a smallpox epidemic that left the Sheffield community relatively unscathed.

It is this early, idyllic period of mutualism between about 1843 and 1847 or '48 that most often serves as an epiphany in the stories I have heard. There are no denouements. What is there at the end is rapture in the face of the teller; an earnest, inquisitive look directed at the listener and a kind of wistfulness I find discomforting.

The story would often seem no more to the teller than an extraordinary history which spoke well of the natural attributes of the country and was naively instructional in the Christian virtues, though one hesitated to be cynical. The various embellishments emphasized, beyond the beauty of the region, ingenuous sharing and cooperation, an absence of violence and a good relationship

with the Quotaka. It is with this that I gradually grew a
little impatient, believing the thread of something important had been lost. Even more distracting to me was
that among all the episodes there were so few that bore
on the Quotaka, or indeed on the profound and central
enigma of Sheffield: one afternoon in 1857 an itinerant
tinsmith found the community deserted. No note of explanation. Signs of local flooding but no other sign of
hardship. No one in the community was ever seen again.

In spite of these difficulties I was from the beginning
taken with these stories, which could be heard in the
cafes and taverns or over dinner in peoples' homes, to
which I was occasionally invited. I confirmed some of
the particulars in libraries and archives. It seemed, from
Alder's journal, which he kept through 1854, and other
documents of the time, that the community did uncom-
monly well. But it also came to an end, and no one I
spoke with wanted to talk about that, or even considered
it important. They only enjoyed the first part of the
story.

The evening Hanner and I walked down the road
together he told me he thought the Sheffield community
had eventually failed, as all such idealistic groups do;
that they were as contentious as any group, as taken with
a sense of cultural primacy and, ultimately, personal
need. The Quotaka interested him more. A Quotaka,
he said, had taught him how to fish.

We walked on in silence. It was on my mind to quiz
Hanner closely on certain points when he began
abruptly to speak.

"The man's name was Elishtanak. When my father
died he came and asked my mother if he could take me
fishing, and he made a regular thing of it. He understood fishing, and that's what he taught me, to understand the obligations and the mutual courtesies involved.
He would sit on the bank of the river with me and talk
about steelhead and chinook as well as anyone who ever
wrote it down. I've fished this river the way he taught

me and fished it better than anyone. And every day I
did it the feeling filled me that I was sure of myself, that
because I understood this I could weather anything.

"Elishtanak told me a story. One time" (Hanner's voice
changed in such a way that the hair went up on the back
of my neck and I leaned forward involuntarily, as
though about to be overtaken by something in the dark)
"before there were any people walking around this valley there were bear people. They had an agreement with
the salmon." Hanner put his fingers to his forehead, as
though coming into a memory of it. "The salmon would
come upriver every fall and the bears would acknowl-
edge this and take what they needed. This is the way it
was with everything. Everyone lived by certain agreements and courtesies. But the salmon people and the
bear people had made no agreement with the river. It
had been overlooked. No one thought it was even necessary. Well, it was. One fall the river pulled itself back
into the shore trees and wouldn't let the salmon enter
from the ocean. Whenever they would try, the river
would pull back and leave the salmon stranded on the
beach. There was a long argument, a lot of talk. Finally
the river let the salmon enter. But when the salmon got
up into this country where the bears lived the river began
to run in two directions at once, north on one side, south
on the other, roaring, heaving, white water, and rolling
big boulders up on the banks. Then the river was suddenly still. The salmon were afraid to move. The bears
were standing behind trees, looking out. The river said
in the middle of all this silence that there had to be an
agreement. No one could just do something, whatever
they wanted. You couldn't just take someone for
granted.

"So for several days they spoke about it. The salmon
said who they were and where they came from, and the
bears spoke about what they did, what powers they had
been given, and the river spoke about its agreement with
the rain and the wind and the crayfish and so on. Every-

body said what they needed and what they would give away. Then a very odd thing happened—the river said it loved the salmon. No one had ever said anything like this before. No one had taken this chance. It was an honesty that pleased everyone. It made for a very deep agreement among them.

"Well they were able to reach an understanding about their obligations to each other and everyone went his way. This remains unchanged. Time has nothing to do with this. This is not a story. When you feel the river shuddering against your legs, you are feeling the presence of all these agreements."

We walked on.

"I think those people at Sheffield just went their separate ways, but maybe they never made an agreement with the river, and the Quotaka hated them so much for it that after the epidemic they never told them you had to do that, and that's what happened. A flood. Quick, in the middle of the night, into their homes. I don't know. You can feel the anger in water behind a dam."

I sensed, off to my left, the moonlit running of the river, heard its muffled voice. We continued down the road, abandoned at this late hour by cars. Hanner looked off into the darkness and I felt an insect land suddenly in my ear.

DAWN

APRICOTS. IT WAS BECAUSE THE WATER SMELLED like apricots as much as anything that she went down to the water. She rose in the darkness and dressed and went down through the trees, trailing her fingers, touching plants she knew but whose names she'd never taken to mind—*syringa*, someone once said, for the mock orange, whose leaves reminded her of silk. *Silkbush*. Rhododendron. Leather-leaved and masculine. Huckleberry. Small leaves stiff with fear. Drops of water from a midnight shower perched on each leaf, resting on the earth grass and broken under her bare feet walking. Mist against her face. Female rain. (Rain in sheets hammering the river, *chuuuuuuush* all afternoon, flattening the riffles, stretching the skin of surface water taut. Male rain.)

She would rise and dress and go down through the trees to the rocks and sit, gather her knees against her chest and smell the metal odor of the water (feel how her pelvis worked against the rock, and the cool wetness of her feet with the dew [female rain] on them and she imagined how wide her eyes must be in the dark), an odor which would change with the light.

Around her in the water, because they could not be seen, had nothing to fear, male mergansers—red feather, blue feather, yellow feather, brown, white feather, white feather, iridescent green—and female

123

mergansers—gray blue, gray blue gray blue gray blue
warrior feather gray blue (twenty-one with her, against
the osprey) and a little maroon. Slept. Ducks slept. Beneath them salmon slept. Beneath them the river un-
dulated, like sun-dried bed linen shaken out in a French
hotel room in the countryside.

While she dreamed of English museums (he wanted
to go on, always, to some other thing), of how to ask a
question, a weasel slipped onto the dark rock, quivering,
nose in the air, neck rammed out stiff. She heard the
crockery sound of water as it flowed around the rocks
and it made her sympathetic. The weasel shot to her,
stopped short, saw the size of her against the stars and
ran.

Europe, she thought, seeing the way someone ate
torte, remembering her fingers on Laocoön's marble calf
in the Vatican, smelling cappuccino, came on a schedule
not hers.

She would come down to the river in the morning
naked under the print dress bought on the road to somewhere (New Mexico: he would know) because she
wanted to cover herself, be covered by this dress, this
loose, fitting loosely this way, and the print of fleur-de-
lis, something small, blue against the off-white exactly.
Cotton. This exactly. Ten dollars. Yes, exactly this. He
didn't like it.

She would go down in the morning through the trees,
touch the leaves of plants whose names she did not know,
naked under the print dress, female rain on the bridge
of her nose.

Above her head (she thought of the female merganser
poised on the rock mid-river, the ducklings around her,
the osprey hidden in shadow high in the cottonwood)
in the limbs of an ash tree a gray owl was taking a weasel
apart. In the east the black was a deeper blue, the color
of the days around her father's death. Exactly. And got
bluer and the water, the river, became visible and black.
She stretched her legs out, matching her calves and arch-

ing her feet, the unfolding beginning there, and with her palms flat on the rock and her head lolling backward she lifted her chest until her spine bent like a bow, shuddered (remembering the osprey motionless in the shadows, watching the merganser and the ducklings huddled on the rock knowing [he had explained all this later] as long as they stayed on the rock, covering it as they did, he would not stoop). And up in the house he rolled over and did not sense that she was gone.

She would go down to the river while it was still dark, and know by the call of the thrushes when it was light enough (opening her eyes, having been at the memory of some cheese like Gouda but with another name in a village [Lyons?] and how he had looked away as though embarrassed when she said sexual, how sexual)—light enough to see the path through the trees. But she went when she went always before dawn, before she could see.

One morning in the gray light, its sound at first submerged in the river's movements, a dory came. A man in a hat rowing. Moving downriver, as foreign as anything she could imagine. Another stood in the bow. He wore another hat and was dressed in neat khaki clothing. She saw the gentle whip of his fly rod pointing into the slack water behind large rocks, after rainbow trout. He looked—exactly the word she was after—silly. But he whipped the rod to set the fly here and there, time and again, the other man rowing, now the rattle of an oarlock, the boat moving toward her, the excessive neatness of their clothing, the creases, the grim expression clear on their red, razor-stropped faces, rowing hard. She froze with the weight of lead in her belly, coming that fast across the water toward her—never saw her, whipping the shallows for fish, went by, thirty feet away. Silly. Her face quivered. Silly. She put her hands, her palms cold from the rock, against her face.

* * *

Winter and summer she would come down to be in the rocks by the water, lying in the dark, waiting for the light, as though by the act itself she could overcome her losses. She meant to remember to tell someone—how the colors came out each morning, how she would like *layers of fabric like this*, a dress where the wind blew each layer open, somehow. In the beginning only the blue blacks, very cool, all the way through to the red of a certain beetle brilliant on her kneecap at ten o'clock, to white Caribbean pastels at noon. Somehow.

She would undress and with sprinkling sounds wash her hands and her face (the osprey, giving up, lifted off the cottonwood limb and flew on upriver, and the merganser, when he was gone, led the ducklings off the rock—twenty-one, she counted them [he said no, that the book said fourteen, tops]—across open water to the protection of overhanging trees along the bank. Had waited him out, staring down at her from the tree, had kept them all still on the rock, never mentioning the osprey, telling a story, telling many stories until he went upriver and she could lead them to the protection of trees along the bank) and slip naked into the water, her orifices closing against the coolness, her skin tightening. The current was too strong and there were too many rocks, clearly visible now, green with moss and stones to bruise her knees in the shallows. She went out from the rock, caught the surge around it and went downstream to a place where she grabbed maple branches and swung around on her belly to face the current. The water lifted her up and when she spread her legs let her down. She closed her eyes and let the water break around her nose and lifted, against her breasts, arched her back, the current against her hips, opened her legs and sank down. She imagined herself among salmon (against her, opened her legs and sank down), swimming gently among salmon (lifting, sank down), until the light seemed much brighter, birds quieter, and she was wide-eyed, afraid of being seen, that the privacy of her morning had broken like an eggshell, and she came out on the bank.

She sat down on the rock in the print dress, the sunlight prickling with the coolness of the river over her and feeling the movement of air over the rock. She dried her eyes with the hem of the dress and saw in the island of hair between her legs suspended—she was overcome with tenderness—two small bits of alder leaf, bright green.

She sat there, damp in the dress, feeling taut in a way that pleased her. She thought of him asleep up there in the house, of how the water (she had told him and he had smiled) at this time in the morning smelled like apricots. Exactly.

UPRIVER

THE COURSE OF THE RIVER ABOVE THE FALLS IS largely unknown, for the climb is arduous and at that point the road passes near and provides a view to satisfy most. The country on up to the headwaters has been walked by government men looking for clues to mineral deposits and to complete maps, but it remains unknown nevertheless. The illusion has been sustained, if one asks around or consults a topographic map, that it is well known; but I know this to be false. And I cannot help but marvel at how little care has been taken in making certain distinctions. For example, at the headwaters itself, farther up than is shown, ravens are meditating, and it is from *them* that the river actually flows, for at night they break down and weep; the universal anguish of creatures, their wailing in desolation, the wrenching anger of betrayals—this seizes them and passes out of them and in that weeping the river takes its shape.

Any act of kindness of which they hear, no matter how filled with trepidation, brings up a single tear, and it, too, runs down the black bills, splashes on small stones and is absorbed in the trickle. Farther along the murmur of fish enters, and the sensation of your hands on sheets of cold steel, the impenetrable wall presented by certain deep shades of blue, the sound of a crack working its way through a plate of English china; this sound, the sound of quick drawn breath, the odor of humus, an

image of the earth hurtling through space with thought
ripped from its surface, left floating like shredded fabric
in its wake, the loss of what is imagined but uncared
for—all this is wound among the tears of bending pain
and moments of complete vulnerability in each of us to
form, finally, visible water, and farther on a creek, lim-
pid and cool, of measurable dimension.

I have in the past recounted these observations to
audiences poorly chosen and have had to move on after
the silent reception, a narrow-eyed, malevolent squint-
ing behind me, as though I were waking to knowledge
of a cobra in a dark room. But this does not disturb me.
The images are irrefutable, requiring only patience to
perceive. They come into view as easily as a book is
hooked with a finger and pulled from a shelf. But perhaps you already know this.

In recent years I have spent considerable time above
the falls, along what I believe to be an unknown section
of the river. It is in some ways the most dangerous country, reverberating with hope, seducing in its simplicity.
It is little traveled. I mean to examine things slowly and
thoroughly there; as often as I have failed at it, gone
running with gleeful intuition toward what seemed an
answer, I have hauled myself back, returned again to a
strict and ordered course. After the initial, difficult sur-
vey I began to examine short sections of the river one
at a time in the hope—beguiling but achingly real—of
a larger vision. I noted, therefore, which creatures fre-
quented each portion of the bank, the kind and number
of riparian plants, the shape and structure of pebbles,
the time of breezes, as well as the small and easily missed
traces of observations not my own. I strove to be complete in my examinations, yet to not lean toward arro-
gance or presumption. In this way I came to a bend in
the river one day from which I could see a house, which
I slowly approached.

It was painted gray, with deep blue shutters in the
Cape Cod style. Four stories pitched against the side of

a steep hill, the windows casement-hung with small panes of leaded glass. A broad porch, on which moved the teasing shadows of tree limbs. My hand took the white porcelain doorknob of a French door. Its glass tempered the light, as I closed it behind me, to the interior of the house. The floors were oak parquet, the rooms spacious with centered rugs of Indonesian hemp, as thick underfoot as moss. The walls were papered in such a way as to appear distant, ghostly, as though seen underwater, at times the light interrupted them altogether. They were—one of the things one remembers for no reason, with which one insulates himself against all that is unknown—Cockerell marbled papers, from England, elegantly designed and of those colors between primary and pastel that burst on you like a forgotten name or the taste of a peach.

The furniture consisted of a few pieces, thoughtfully placed. A chair or two, often set alone by a window, as though someone had been watching, had just stepped into another room, was listening now in a stillness that suggested canyons or regret. A woman's bed, with a brass bedstead and a spread of soft chenille, white as sun-bleached seashells, on which, somehow, light was always falling and on which she and I would lie, trusting, and fall asleep in the afternoon.

In one or two of the rooms were tables, of the sort one might choose to sit alone at to write a letter. I would sit and watch the river move through the trees, my hands folded on the table or cupped in my lap, with a look (she would say) of dismay and acceptance.

We would dance. We would remove our shoes and with only that slight chirp of skin against the oak floor we would dance to an imagined music until we were brought around by a movement of wind through the house and in our ecstasy another rhythm: songs remembered from springs of celebration in country close by, where the oaks grew once, implacable, hosting sparrows, rising now out of the floor as though released again. In moments of vulnerability such as this we would not speak and hardly move. Strands of her hair stuck to my cheek, the sound of our breathing. Out of respect for the floor.

The trees outside barely moved, thoughts passing sub rosa leaf to leaf.

In a room I entered for the first time one fall I found a book. It was left open on the window sill, as though someone would return. It was printed in a language I do not know which I nevertheless read, page by page, as though sensing a promise in the very form of the words and sentences and the feel of the chapter breaks of imminent revelation. None was forthcoming and I abandoned this project.

We danced, most often. And in the evening I would tell stories. The way we desired each other became dance and stories, and the passion took us as deeply, left us embracing and protective.

In that time I do not remember ever being away, though I know I was. Even now in the memory of it I do not know where I am. I know that I still spend time in the upper part of the river and that those relationships I hold to be true, such as that between anguish and the birth of rivers, endure.

Farther up the river are the unfolding of other relationships, together with the loss of the promise of anything to be found. I have been led to believe that that is the reason no one goes up that far, though the promise, in its way, is kept. It is the walk home that is terrifying.

DROUGHT

I AWOKE ONE NIGHT AND THOUGHT I HEARD RAIN—
it was the dry needles of fir trees falling on the roof.
Men with an intolerable air of condolence have appeared, as though drawn by the smell of death, dressed
comfortably, speaking a manipulated tongue, terminally
evil. They have inquired into the purchase of our homes.
And reporters come and go, outraged over the absence
of brown trout, which have never been here. The river
like some great whale lies dying in the forest.

In the years we have been here I have trained myself
to listen to the river, not in the belief that I could understand what it said, but only from one day to the next
know its fate. The river's language arose principally
from two facts: the slightest change in its depth brought
it into contact with a different portion of the stones along
its edges and the rocks and boulders mid-stream that
lay in its way, and so changed its tone; and although its
movement around one object may seem uniform at any
one time it is in fact changeable. Added to these major
variations are the landings of innumerable insects on its
surface, the breaking of its waters by fish, the falling
into it of leaves and twigs, the slooshing of raccoons, the
footfalls of deer; ultimately these are only commentary
on the river's endless reading of the surface of the earth
over which it flows.

It was in this way that I learned before anyone else

of the coming drought. Day after day as the river fell by imperceptible increments its song changed, notes came that were unknown to me. I mentioned this to no one, but each morning when I awoke I went immediately to the river's edge and listened. It was as though I could hear the sound rain begins to make in a country where it is not going to come for a long time.

As the water fell, however, nothing unexpected was uncovered, although the effect of standing in areas once buried beneath the roar of the river's current was unsettling. I found only one made object, a wheel, the kind you find on the back of a child's tricycle. But I didn't look as closely as the others. The wailing of the river over its last stones was difficult to bear, yet it was this that drew me back each day, as one visits those dying hopelessly in a hospital room. During those few hours each morning I would catch stranded fish barehanded in shallow pools and release them where the river still flowed. The bleaching of algae once waving green underwater to white; river stones once cool now hot to the touch and dry; spider webs stretched where there had been salmon eggs; snakes where there had been trout— it was as though the river had been abandoned.

During those summer days, absorbed with the death of the river and irritated at the irreverent humor of weather forecasters in distant cities, I retreated into a state of isolation. I fasted and abstained as much as I felt appropriate from water. These were only gestures, of course, but even as a boy I knew a gesture might mean life or death and I believed the universe was similarly triggered.

From this point on, the song that came out of the river did not bother me as much. I sat out of the way of the pounding sun, in dark rocks shaded by the overhanging branches of alders along the bank. Their dry leaves, stirred by the breeze, fell brittle and pale around me. I slept on the bank regularly now. I would say very simple prayers in the evening, only an expression of camaraderie, stretching my fingers gently into the darkness toward the inchoate source of the river's strangulation. I did not beg. There was a power to dying, and it should be done with grace. I was only making a gesture on the shore, a speck in the steep, brutal dryness of the valley by a dying river.

In moments of great depression, of an unfathomable compassion in myself, I would make the agonized and tentative movements of a dance, like a long-legged bird. I would exhort the river.

What death we saw. Garter snake stiff as a twig in the rocks. Trees (young ones, too young) crying out in the night, shuddering, dropping all their leaves. Farther from the river, birds falling dead in thickets, animals dead on the paths, their hands stiffened in gestures of bewilderment and beseeching; the color gone out of the eyes of any creature you met, for whom, out of respect, you would step off the path to allow to pass.

Where a trickle of water still flowed there was an atmosphere of truce, more dangerous than one might imagine. As deer and coyote sipped from the same tiny pool they abrogated their agreement, and the deer contemplated the loss of the coyote as he would the loss of a friend; for the enemy, like the friend, made you strong. I was alert for such moments, for they were augury, but I was as wary of them as of any lesson learned in death.

One moonlit evening I dreamed of a certain fish. The fish was gray-green against light-colored stones at the bottom of a deep pool, breathing a slow, unperturbed breathing, the largest fish I had ever imagined living in the river. The sparkling of the water around him and the sound of it cascading over the creek bed made me weak and I awoke suddenly, convulsed. I knew the fish. I knew the place. I set out immediately.

The dry riverbed was only a clatter of teetering stones now, ricocheting off my feet as I passed, bone weary, feeling disarmed by hunger, by the dimness of the night,

and by the irrefutable wisdom and utter foolishness of
what I was doing. As I drew near the mouth of the creek
the fish began to loom larger and larger and I could
feel—as though my hands were extended to a piece of
cloth flapping in the darkness—both the hope and the
futility of such acts.

I found the spot where the creek came in and went
up it. I had seen the fish once in a deep pool below a
rapids where he had fed himself too well and grown too
large to escape. There was a flow of night air coming
down the creek bed, rattling dry leaves. In the faint
moonlight a thousand harlequin beetles suddenly settled
on my clothing and I knew how close I was to a loss of
conviction, to rage, to hurling what beliefs I had like a
handful of pebbles into the bushes.

The beetles clung to the cloth, moved through my
hair, came into the cups of my hands as I walked, and
as suddenly were gone, and the area I stood in was
familiar, the fish before me. The rapids were gone. The
pool had become a pit. In its lowest depression the huge
fish lay motionless, but for the faint lifting of a gill cover.
I climbed down to him and wrapped him in my shirt,
soaked in the pool. I had expected, I think, a fight, to
be punched in that pit by the fish who lay in my arms
now like a cold lung.

Climbing out of there, stopping wherever I could to
put his head under in some miserable pool, hurrying, I
came to the river and the last trickle of water, where I
released him without ceremony.

I knew, as I had known in the dream, the danger I
was in but I knew, too, that without such an act of self-
assertion no act of humility had meaning.

By now the river was only a whisper. I stood at the
indistinct edge and exhorted what lay beyond the river,
which now seemed more real than the river itself. With
no more strength than there is in a bundle of sticks I
tried to dance, to dance the dance of the long-legged

birds who lived in the shallows. I danced it because I could not think of anything more beautiful.

The turning came during the first days of winter. Lynx came down from the north to what was left of the river. Deer were with him. And from some other direction Raccoon and Porcupine. And from downriver Weasel and White-footed Mouse, and from above Blue Heron and Goshawk. Badger came up out of the ground with Mole. They stood near me in staring silence and I was afraid to move. Finally Blue Heron spoke: "We were the first people here. We gave away all the ways of living. Now no one remembers how to live anymore, so the river is drying up. Before we could ask for rain there had to be someone to do something completely selfless, with no hope of success. You went after that fish, and then at the end you were trying to dance. A person cannot be afraid of being foolish. For everything, every gesture, is sacred.

"Now, stand up and learn this dance. It is going to rain."

We danced together on the bank. And the songs we danced to were the river songs I remembered from long ago. We danced until I could not understand the words but only the sounds, and the sounds were unmistakably the sound rain makes when it is getting ready to come into a country.

I awoke in harsh light one morning, moved back into the trees and fell asleep again. I awoke later to what I thought were fir needles falling on my cheeks but these were drops of rain.

It rained for weeks. Not hard, but steadily. The river came back easily. There were no floods. People said it was a blessing. They offered explanations enough. Backs were clapped, reputations lost and made, the seeds of future argument and betrayal sown, wounds suffered and allowed, pride displayed. It was no different from any other birth but for a lack of joy and, for that, stranger than anything you can imagine, inhuman and presumptuous. But people go their way, and with reason; and the hardness for some is all but unfathomable, and so begs forgiveness. Everyone has to learn how to die, that song, that dance, alone and in time.

The river has come back to fit between its banks. To stick your hands into the river is to feel the cords that bind the earth together in one piece. The sound of it at a distance is like wild horses in a canyon, going surefooted away from the smell of a cougar come to them faintly on the wind.

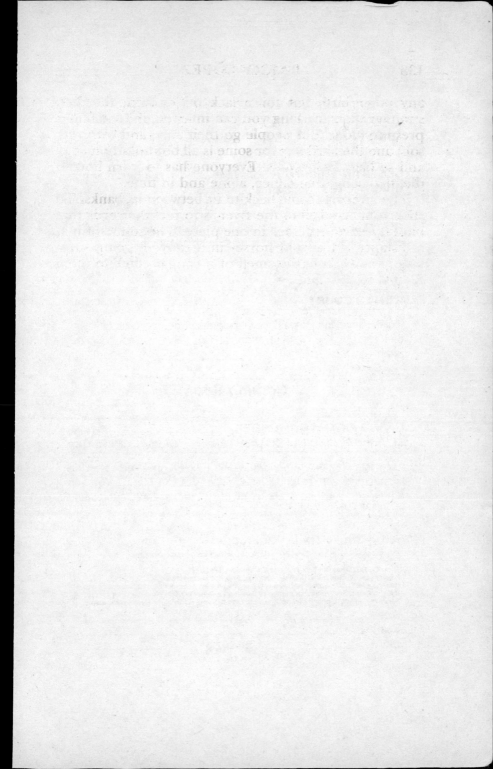